# Praise for Life After the State

'Dominic Frisby has gone and done something extraordinary: written a page-turner on the economy. It's both readable and radical, a serious book that is, by turn, fascinating, alarming and contentious. At times, the book makes you want to shout its message from the rooftops; at others, it just makes you want to shout. Life After the State challenges so much of what we take for granted. It is a wake-up call for politicians, economists and us all, written with clarity, verve and, more than that, the restless passion of an intelligent, inquisitive malcontent. Read it.'
James Harding, BBC Director of News and Current Affairs

'Congratulations on your brilliant book ... it will do more good than all my speeches in Parliament and around the country.'
Steve Baker, MP

'It's incredibly readable and incredibly thought-provoking.'
Al Murray, The Pub Landlord

'An entertaining cogent attack on state power, which should topple the centralist Trots once and for all.'
Tom Hodgkinson, The Idler

'Thought-provoking and original, anyone concerned how big and bloated government has become must read this book.'
Douglas Carswell, MP

'Things are so bad that in our time only a comedian can make sense of an economy based on printing money.'
Guido Fawkes, political blogger

'If you're still keen on revolution, give Brand a miss and have a read of some genuinely fresh ideas from Dominic Frisby – his book Life After the State ... will give you a lot more food for thought than anything Brand trots out.'
John Stepek, editor, MoneyWeek

'Clear, honest and arguably difficult for an acclaimed economist to mimic ... The implications for education, healthcare, enterprise and thereby the general well being of society are clearly profound.'
Amazon reviewer

'This is a well-researched and referenced work, and despite its radical thesis deserves to have a place alongside other serious books on economics and politics. Unlike many of them though, it is readable, entertaining and inspiring. I would even go as far as to say this is a book that could change the world.'
Amazon reviewer

'The greatest tribute that I can give to Dominic and his book is that my darling wife, who usually falls asleep as soon as the subject of economics comes up, read his book from cover to cover in a single sitting and was most impressed by it. Thank you Dominic.'
Amazon reviewer

'Quite simply it's one of the best, informative, intelligent reads I've ever had. Don't hesitate, just buy it, read it, and see how our modern world works, or rather doesn't work, with clearer eyes.'
Amazon reviewer

'This work is revelatory and is essential reading – I wish I had had it available as a young man. I have given copies to each of my children (over 16) and hope they read it – it will make life so much more understandable to them.'
Amazon reviewer

'The most important book I have read in a long time. I've just bought five extra copies, and plan to force it on all I meet, in the manner of a Jehovah's Witness.'
Amazon reviewer

# ABOUT THE AUTHOR

Dominic Frisby is, unusually, both a comedian and financial writer.

As a comedian he has been described as 'viciously funny and inventive' by the *Guardian*; 'very impressive and very witty' by *The Times* and 'masterful' by the *Evening Standard*. But his first book, *Life After the State*, had nothing to do with comedy. Published by Unbound in 2013 to critical acclaim, it is a deadly-serious dismantling of the way societies are run in the West.

Dominic writes an investment column for *MoneyWeek* and has made numerous popular YouTube videos, including the viral hit 'Debt Bomb'. He has also worked as a TV presenter, a boxing-ring announcer, a florist, a removal man, an extremely camp theatrical agent's PA, a sports commentator and a busker. He is a voiceover artist and is an in-demand speaker.

*Bitcoin: The Future of Money?* is his second book.

*With special thanks to Carl Holt*

# BITCOIN

# BITCOIN

The Future Of Money?

## Dominic Frisby

unbound

This edition first published in 2014

10 9 8 7 6 5 4 3 2

Unbound

4–7 Manchester Street, Marylebone, London, W1U 2AE

www.unbound.co.uk

Typeset by Unbound

Cover design by Mecob

A CIP record for this book is available from the British Library

ISBN 978-1-78352-077-0

ISBN 978-1-78352-076-3 (ebook)

Printed in England by Clays Ltd, Bungay, Suffolk

*As always*
*For Samuel, Eliza, Lola and Ferdie.*
*I love you all more than life itself.*

*For*
*Brian Cartmell,*
*Duncan Black*
*and*
*Wade Smith.*

*And, of course, for*
*Satoshi Nakamoto.*

*Pure anonymity provides voice for a wide variety of new kinds of expression that up until now have been suppressed.*

Nick Szabo, computer scientist and blogger

# Contents

# AUTHOR'S NOTE

I have called this book *Bitcoin: The Future of Money?* Really, I should have called it *Cryptocurrency: The Future of Money?*

Bitcoin is just one of many cryptocurrencies (don't worry, I'll explain what that means). It is, arguably, not even the first. But it is the first that works. And it is the one that has caught everyone's attention. Rather as people say 'Scotch tape' or 'Sellotape' instead of 'sticky-back plastic', Bitcoin is the name everybody knows – hence my choice of title.

I have quoted extensively from online forums and chat boards. These often contain spelling mistakes and grammatical errors. For the sake of accuracy, I have made the decision to leave these errors uncorrected. Nor have I acknowledged errors with a 'sic', as I felt this would be both patronizing to those I quote and burdensome on the reader. So, when you come across errors in quoted passages, now you know why.

In researching this book, I have come across entire political and technological movements I'd never even heard of, filled with characters I knew even less about. They might be infamous to a small band of computer coders, but not to most people. What's more, those who discuss Bitcoin and its associated technology quickly slip into technical jargon, particularly regarding computer code. It can make it all rather baffling and, worse still, alienating. If you think finance and economics are hard to write about in a clear way, try computer code with an all-star cast whose names mean absolutely nothing to most people.

I've tried to make it all as clear and concise as possible – to tell this amazing story in such a way that you don't have to be a 25-year-old computer hacker to understand it – but nor will you be bored if you are one. To get the balance right, I have had it read, at one end of the scale, by numerous computer programmers and, at the other, by my 82-year-old, technologically illiterate dad.

I hope you enjoy it.

# PROLOGUE

*We have not only saved the world, er, saved the banks...*
— Gordon Brown, former UK Prime Minister

In September 2008, crisis gripped the world.

Many believed the entire financial system was about to collapse. It was a 'global financial tsunami'; we were 'on the brink' and 'staring into the abyss'.[1] Capitulating stock markets, bankruptcies, bank runs – events came thick and fast and, at first, nobody seemed to know quite what to do.

Then, under immense pressure from the world of finance, governments and central banks reacted dramatically. They created money and credit on a scale unprecedented in human history. Banks were bailed out, interest rates were slashed to levels never seen before and the process of creating money electronically known as quantitative easing was begun.

The result?

The financial system was saved. Central bankers were hailed as heroes. The idea spread that governments and central banks really can operate an economy. Even those who would normally oppose such interventions seemed to think the right thing had been done.

A few dissenters argued that the few were being bailed

out at the expense of the many, that enormous problems in the financial system were simply being deferred when they needed to be faced, and that these problems would only come back on a far greater scale. At the heart of the problem is *money itself*, they said. The way money is created means that banks and governments have inordinate control over our financial system. They profit hugely by it, while everybody else loses. The system actually creates inequality.

But such dissent was ignored – if, indeed, it was even heard.

'Only a crisis, real or perceived, produces real change', said economist Milton Friedman. Here was that opportunity for real change – an opportunity to reform our systems of money, banking and finance – our entire economies even. Politicians chose not to take it, preferring instead to save a broken system.

But that badly needed change was taking place – secretly, in a remote corner of the internet, far away from the sound and fury of this great financial crisis.

On August 18th 2008, a domain name is registered – bitcoin.org.

Even today, nobody knows who registered it.

Two weeks later, one Satoshi Nakamoto publishes a nine-page white paper outlining a design for 'Bitcoin: A Peer-To-Peer Electronic Cash System'.[2] Nobody takes any notice.

Two months pass. On November 1st 2008, with the stock market now in full-on crash mode, Satoshi mentions his paper on a mailing list for people with an interest in cryptography.

'I've been working on a new electronic cash system that's fully peer-to-peer, with no trusted third party',[3] he says.

Readers throw him various technical questions, which he answers. Nobody seems persuaded. It does not 'scale to the required size', says one. The code 'can't work on today's internet', says another. Governments will close it down if it takes off, says a third.

'I believe I've worked through all those little details over the last year and a half while coding it, and there were a lot of them', says Satoshi. 'I appreciate your questions. I actually did this kind of backwards. I had to write all the code before I could convince myself that I could solve every problem'.[4]

A week later the Bitcoin project is registered at Source-forge, a website 'dedicated to making open source projects successful'.[5]

On Saturday January 3rd 2009, the day UK Chancellor Alistair Darling announces his second bailout of the banks, the first 50 bitcoins are created – or, to use the correct terminology, 'mined'. A few days later, Satoshi returns to the mailing list and says, 'Announcing the first release of Bitcoin, a new electronic cash system.'

What had been born was a new form of money – money that could change the world.

# 1

# WHAT **IS** BITCOIN? HOW IS IT **MADE?**

*Cash is king.*

— Stock market saying

It was probably the greatest trade in all of recorded history.

In October 2009, a Bitcoin aficionado who went by the name of 'Liberty Standard' published the first bitcoin exchange rate. He arrived at the figure by dividing the cost of the electricity consumed by his computer over a 30-day period by the number of bitcoins it generated. 1,309 bitcoins to one dollar was the price.[6] Liberty Standard was actually criticized for valuing bitcoins too high.

Four years later, on November 29th 2013, one bitcoin was $1,242 – over 1.6 million times higher. A bitcoin was the same price as an ounce of gold.

If anybody managed to buy the low (which actually came in December 2009 at 1,630 bitcoins to the dollar) and sell the high, they made over two million times their money. In four years, one dollar became two million dollars.

Nice work if you can get it.

The story of Bitcoin is amazing – not just for the gains (and the losses) that have been made, not just because of the revolutionary technology, but also because of the human stories that have come about as a result.

There's the developer in Finland who, trying out the tech, bought a beer from his buddy for some bitcoins. Three years later, his buddy sold those coins and bought a des res apartment in the trendiest district in Helsinki. There's the computer nerd with an interest in economics who became the FBI's most wanted drug dealer. And, of course, there's the great whodunit.

Who invented Bitcoin? Who is Satoshi Nakamoto?

He has a Japanese name, a German email address and he uses British spelling. He has invented a new form of money that could change the world. He is worth almost a billion dollars. He has computer programmers the world over purring at the unhackable genius of his tech. Half the internet – as well as investigative journalists and forensic scientists, even – have been trying to figure out his identity for over three years. And yet still, nobody knows who he is.

I think I've cracked that, by the way.

The story of Bitcoin has everything from the hilarious to the mysterious to the audacious to the calamitous.

Genius computer hackers. Dogs with funny names. Cypherpunks. Cryptography. Financial systems. Governments. Organized crime. Attempted murder. Political insurrection. Inspiring bursts of generosity. Squatters. Poker players. City traders. And people just like you.

# How Bitcoin could change everything

Everybody is constantly thinking about ways to make money.

The average American spends more hours of each day attempting to earn it than he does anything else[7] – be that eating, playing or even sleeping.

But hardly a soul – not even highbrow economists – stops to consider what money actually is and how it works.

It is hard to overstate how important money is. Like the air we breathe, it is part of almost everything we do. Just about every transaction we make involves money. To use another analogy, what blood is to a body, money is to an economy.

Governments, central banks and private banks create modern money – dollars, pounds, euros and so on. This ability to create money is – as I'm sure you appreciate – an immensely powerful privilege. While most have treated this privilege responsibly most of the time, there are plenty that haven't. And all sorts of abuses have crept in.

Politicians are forever spending more money than they have – aka running up deficits – in pursuit of some ideology or political agenda (normally popularity and re-election). They might spend the money on bailing out banks, on welfare, on some kind of subsidy; they might even spend it on wars (the US military is the world's biggest employer). Central banks manipulate interest rates and inflation numbers on behalf of politicians and special interest groups. Private banks, through such means as lending and leverage, perpetrate their own abuses in pursuit of profit. As a result of all this, money gets debased.

Government agencies even use money as a means to control people and spy on them.

Money is supposed to be a means of exchange and a store of wealth, but it is also a political tool. This has been the case throughout history, but the control of governments and banks has grown over the last hundred years and is now unprecedented. It has led to huge concentrations of wealth and power. Both the state and finance now occupy, in the eyes of many, disproportionate territory in our economies.

Meanwhile, over half the world's population still doesn't have access to basic financial services and is shut out.

Suddenly, along comes Bitcoin, an open-source currency with no central authority, offering an alternative that could undermine the existing monetary order. Nobody even knows who designed it. It's by no means the first attempt at digital cash, but it's the first that works this well. It's actually more efficient than dollars or pounds. It's immune to all the manipulation and abuses that go on, there are no barriers to entry, bar internet access, and it has captured a zeitgeist in a way that nobody could have foreseen.

If Bitcoin changes the way we transact and the way we store wealth – and it has the potential to do this – the repercussions could be enormous. Think what email did to the postal service, or what the internet did to newspapers, publishing, music and television. With the huge costs involved in the printing and distribution of physical newspapers, news publishing was once the exclusive domain of a few large companies. Now any blogger, aspiring journalist or start-up can publish on the web, effectively for free. Huge opportunities have opened up to the masses, and the old dinosaurs have seen their monopolies eroded.

We're still a long way from that, but Bitcoin could do something similar to banking, finance and, even, the large state model under which we live. Without wishing to get too excited, it could bring about the huge changes to society so many are clamouring for, re-balancing the skewed distribution of wealth and opportunity. The implications are enormous.

That's why Bitcoin is important.

## What is Bitcoin?

When you type a website address into a browser you might have noticed that the letters 'http' appear at the front. 'Http' stands for Hypertext Transfer Protocol. In typing an address you are actually sending an HTTP command to transmit that website to you. Hypertext Transfer Protocol is the means by which information is shared across the web.

Similarly, when setting up an email account, you might have noticed the letters 'smtp' – for example, 'smtp.gmail.com'. SMTP stands for Simple Mail Transfer Protocol. SMTP is the protocol by which we send emails to each other. What actually happens when you send an email through Gmail to, say, someone with a Yahoo address is that a Google server reaches out to a Yahoo server and transmits a text file; then the Yahoo server says to its user, 'you've got mail'.

So, a protocol is an agreed system by which information is shared across a network.

Bitcoin – with a capital 'B' – is another protocol. The function of the protocol is to send and receive payment information.

With Bitcoin, your computer reaches out to another user's computer, gives it some binary gibberish proving you control X number of coins at this address and want them to increase the balance at that address.

The unit of money on the Bitcoin protocol is the 'bitcoin' (with a small 'b'). As the dollar is the unit of money on the US banking network, so bitcoin is the unit of money on the Bitcoin system.

So, Bitcoin is two things – a protocol and a unit of money.

## How do you get bitcoins?

Using dollars or pounds is easy.

You get paid in them. They're in your bank account (hopefully). And you can pay for things with them via electronic banking, by cheque, credit card, or in cash.

But where on earth do you get bitcoins?

There are three ways.

You can *get paid* in bitcoins. You can *buy* bitcoins. And last of all (the very unconventional bit), you can *make* bitcoins. Yes, you can, literally, create money.

You earn bitcoins by doing or selling something in exchange for bitcoins – just as you would earn normal money. If I do this job for you, you pay me in bitcoins.

You buy bitcoins just as you would buy and sell foreign currency – from the Bitcoin equivalent of a *bureau de change*, known as a Bitcoin exchange, or directly from an individual. You hand over your dollars, pounds or whatever currency you're using and you receive bitcoins.

To create bitcoins, you run the Bitcoin software on your computer. It's called 'mining' – more on that later. But I should say that mining has now progressed to the point at which regular home computers are no longer much good.

Of course, you need somewhere to keep your money. You could keep your dollars in a bank account, your back pocket, your wallet or purse, even under your mattress. Bitcoins are kept in a 'digital wallet'.

There are hundreds of places to get a wallet, just as there are hundreds of places to get an email account. Often people will have more than one. You can keep a wallet on your computer or your phone, you could keep one on a hard drive off-line, or you could keep one with an exchange. Some people with lots of bitcoins keep them in a wallet on a hard drive in a safe.

Each wallet has its own address – a sequence of different numbers and letters. To make a payment, you click on your wallet, type in the number of coins you wish to pay, copy and paste the payee's wallet address, hit send and the payment is made. To receive a payment in bitcoins, all the person paying needs is your wallet address. When you receive a payment, your computer might give you a little 'ching' sound to notify you. It is as simple as sending an email.

With barcodes you can open your wallet on your smartphone, photograph the barcode, hit send and the payment is made. The day is not far off when you will walk into a shop, select an item you wish to buy, photograph the code on the label, payment will be made automatically and off you go.

Once you get the hang of it, it is as simple as using a credit card. And, as long as you have internet access, there are no barriers to entry.

## Cash in my wallet, money in the bank

I bet you use different kinds of money all the time, sometimes without even realising it.

In various online accounts, I currently have: some dollars, some pounds and some euros. I have some air miles from two different credit card companies. I have some supermarket rewards points from three different companies. In addition, I have some bitcoins in a wallet on my computer.

These are all tokens with some kind of value, which can be swapped for goods or services. They are all, in other words, different forms of money – nine in total.

Of course, the dollars are more widely accepted than my supermarket rewards points – they are a more effective form of money. But those supermarket reward points are still exchangeable for goods and services of some kind and therefore are also a form of money.

What's more, I have none of these monies on my person. They are all stored and transacted on some computer somewhere – they are all forms of *digital money*.

If I want to exchange the supermarket rewards points or the air miles for some kind of good or service, I must do it through the issuer.

I can send you the dollars, pounds or euros, but I have to do it through a bank.

If I had those dollars, pounds or euros in cash on my person and you were standing next to me, I could hand you that money directly. But most of the people or companies with whom we transact today are not in our immediate vicinity, so we have to send the money via a bank or even a courier.

Making payments this way can be costly, particularly payments abroad or for small amounts. Western Union, for example, can charge as much as 10% of the total money transferred.

There is also the issue of privacy – the bank and people who work for it can see how much money you have, what you buy with it, who you buy from – and what your entire spending habits are.

There is also the issue of risk. The courier could be robbed, the bank could go bust (in theory at least) and so on. It is also worth remembering that money deposited in the bank becomes the property of the bank; it is no longer yours – a fact the majority of people are not aware of.

Also, not everyone in the world has a bank account. While over 90% of adults in first world countries do, in poor countries that number falls to about 40%.[8] Sixty per cent of people in poor countries, in other words, have no access to basic financial services and thus are excluded from the financial system.

But here's the key: with internet access, I can send a bitcoin directly to you with no intermediary, just as I could hand you a note if you were standing next to me. A bitcoin transaction is direct, frictionless and private.

In other words, unlike the dollars, the air miles and all those other forms of money, the bitcoin is *digital cash*.

Digital cash.

The possibilities are endless.

# One of the biggest mysteries of our time: where money comes from

Most people have no idea where money comes from.

Even those who think they do know are usually wrong.

Once upon a time, of course, we used metal as money – gold, silver, nickel and copper. We've also used items as varied as shells, cocoa beans, whales' teeth, even salt (from where we derive the word 'salary'). These 'commodity currencies' all occurred naturally and had a cost of production to them. You had to mine the metal, grow the beans, collect the shells and so on.

Gradually, pieces of paper representing gold or silver stored in a vault were preferred to the actual metal, though you could swap that piece of paper for actual gold if you wanted. This was 'representative currency'. During the time of the gold standard, laws would, eventually, limit the privilege of issuing representative notes to the central bank. However, money was still based on gold and silver and so it still had a cost of production.

In 1914, France, Germany and the UK came off the gold standard. In other words, it was ruled that those pieces of paper money issued by the central bank could no longer be swapped for gold. Now it was the law, rather than gold and silver, which gave money its value. You had to accept this paper in payment of debt. And, because it was now just paper, money had a minimal cost of production.

In 1971, the US followed this same path to fiat money – 'fiat' meaning by government command. Effectively, governments had granted themselves the right to create money for nothing, a right they did not previously enjoy. The age of the large state in which we now live would quickly follow.

Over the last 30 years, however, those government pieces of paper have been used less and less. With electronic banking, which began in the early 1980s, money has become digital or electronic. With this change, the power and influence of banks has grown.

In the US, there are currently about 1.3 trillion dollars in existence in the form of bills and coins.[9] Some are held in banks, some by companies, and some by individuals. Those 1.3 trillion dollars of printed notes equate to just 8% of all US dollars.[10] But many of those printed notes have been lost or destroyed and between half and two-thirds are estimated to be abroad,[11] so it is now thought that just 3% of the US dollars in existence are in physical form in the US.

In the UK, there is a similar story: 3–4% of money in banks and building societies exists in physical form.[12]

Governments have coined or printed the 3–4% of money that is physical cash. But the remaining 96–7% of money is almost all created by banks. Contrary to what most people believe, it is not the government and the central bank that make most of our money. It's banks.

Many people shake their head incredulously at this. How on earth can it be?

Well, banks (not central banks, but so-called 'private banks'; the likes of HSBC or Wells Fargo) create money when they make loans. Consider the sale of my house. The purchasers took on a mortgage to buy it, as is normal. In issuing the mortgage (for which they took the deeds of the house as collateral), the lending bank created money, which was then paid to me. The funds didn't come from investors or from the deposits of others. The money did not previously exist.

Thus modern electronic money – dollars, pounds and euros – is created through lending. Of course, governments create money through such processes as quantitative easing, but, even so, most money is lent into existence. This power to 'create' money through lending is what has made the worlds of banking and finance so large, powerful and rich.

Modern money could thus be defined as 'electronic debt-based fiat currency'.

Research by UK think tank Positive Money shows that since 1989, money creation has been growing by 11.5% per annum. Compounded over time, the entire money stock doubles every six years and three months. This used to be what we called inflation, but modern measures of inflation now ignore money supply and instead focus on the prices of certain goods.

The morals of such a system – where certain privileged groups get to create money – are dubious. The system has, as I argue in depth in *Life After the State*, created all sorts of inequalities across society, chief among them the wealth gap. But, because money supply growth is no longer considered important, many of the causes of inequality go undetected, while the proposed cures are misdiagnosed.

The shortcomings of our money systems are something that Satoshi was attempting to address when he designed Bitcoin:

> The root problem with conventional currency is all
> the trust that's required to make it work. The central
> bank must be trusted not to debase the currency, but

the history of fiat currencies is full of breaches of that trust. Banks must be trusted to hold our money and transfer it electronically, but they lend it out in waves of credit bubbles with barely a fraction in reserve. We have to trust them with our privacy, trust them not to let identity thieves drain our accounts. Their massive overhead costs make micropayments impossible.[13]

Discounting trust, Satoshi set out to design a system of money based on 'proof instead.'[14]

Cryptographic proof.

## The science at which Gandalf the Grey was a master

You send a letter to a friend. The contents of that letter are between you and your friend – you don't want the postman or anyone else reading your letter – so you seal it in an envelope.

A man is in a restaurant with his wife. A waiter is standing at their table. The wife wants to tell her husband something, but without the waiter knowing. She nudges him under the table or gives him a secret look.

Pursued by the nine black riders of Mordor, Gandalf needs to get a message to Frodo and Strider. The future of Middle Earth is at stake. He leaves some runes on a pile of stones on Mount Weathertop.

We are discussing the practice of secure communication between parties within the presence, but without the understanding, of third parties. When such communication takes place electronically, and confidentiality is desired – perhaps it is a communication between you and your bank, and you don't want internet service providers, crooks or the NSA to know what's being said – some sort of encryption software is used. As you can imagine, the role of encryption in the computer age is enormous.

The science of encoding and decoding data to maintain privacy is the science of cryptography. And remember, when Satoshi Nakamoto first announced Bitcoin, he did it on a mailing list only read by people with an interest in cryptography.

## The primitive tropical island that would become a blueprint for Bitcoin

The tiny tropical island of Yap lies in the eastern Pacific Ocean, about a thousand miles to the east of the Philippines. It is about 38 square miles.

Many hundreds of years ago, voyagers, led by a man named Anagumang, travelled some 300 miles from Yap to its closest neighbour, the island of Panau. There they found a kind of limestone rock, rather like marble – calcite rock to be precise – which they had never seen before. It was white, translucent and it sparkled in the sun. They were transfixed by what they saw. Using stone tools and shells, they quarried some of the rock and brought it home.

Back on Yap, the shiny rock was a big hit. People wore it as jewellery and expeditions soon set out to retrieve more of it. Its beauty, its scarcity and the great risks involved in bringing it home (300 miles by canoe) made it extremely precious to the Yapese – just as gold and silver were to people elsewhere in the world.

Deals were struck with the Palau-ans. For the privilege of quarrying their rock, the Yapese paid them beads, coconut meat (copra), even sea cucumbers. They also did jobs for them.

As the rest of the world moved from using gold and silver as jewellery to using it as money, so the Yapese – who had no precious metal – started using this stone as money. It was cut into disc shapes – like coins, in many ways, although considerably bigger. Most were about a foot to two feet in diameter, although they could get as large as five feet across. Holes were cut through the middle of the discs, giving them the look of large doughnuts, so they could be carried on a bamboo pole. They are now known as Rai stones.

They were transported back to Yap on rafts, towed by canoes with sails. During the summer months when the winds and currents were favourable, unmanned rafts were pushed out to sea carrying their valuable stone cargo. Of course, many of them would not make it back to Yap.

The more gold there is in a coin the more valuable it is. The more of this rock there was in a Rai stone the more it was worth. When European travellers arrived in the 19th century with larger ships and iron tools, the stones got even bigger. The largest that made it across the water is found on a small island to the north of Yap, called Rumung. It is almost ten feet across and a foot in width. Weighing several tonnes, it would take over 100 men to lift (it takes about 40 men to lift one tonne).

The Rai stones were the biggest, heaviest, least portable currency in all human history.

The largest stone has been found where it was abandoned back on Palau. It weighs some seven-and-a-half tonnes and is almost 12 feet across. It is also broken. And therein lies one of the problems with this stone cash. Not only were many of the rocks too big to be constantly moved about as you might move around gold, silver or any other form of money, they could also break easily. So the larger stones were simply left in prominent positions in villages and outside people's homes as displays of wealth.

Rather than move the stone each time a transaction took place, the stone was left where it was and ownership of the stone was transferred. The ownership was recorded orally and retained in locals' memory.

Picture an enormous Rai stone sitting prominently in a village. Everyone in the village knows the stone and who it belongs to. Of course this stone wouldn't be used for everyday transactions, but perhaps the owner gives it to someone else as part of a dowry, or a political deal. Perhaps it is inherited. The stone doesn't move. But the villagers will all now know the stone belongs to someone else.

Many of the stones that were quarried in Palau never actually made it all the way to Yap, particularly when travelling by unmanned raft. Many would sink. There is even one story of a crew making it to within a mile of Yap before a storm sunk both the canoes and the rock-laden rafts they were carrying. On one of the rafts was a particularly large stone, which was now lying at the bottom of the sea, miles off the coast. Even this stone, and other sunken stones besides, would be traded, with ownership of the stone recorded orally in the same way as ownership of the stones that were visible in the villages. You know that stone that sunk three years ago and is lying on the ocean floor? That's Gary's.

There are all sorts of parallels between this primitive system of Yap and the idea at the core of Bitcoin.

Bitcoins stay on the internet, just as Rai stones stay where they stand. But with each transaction that takes place, ownership of those bitcoins changes. That ownership is recorded on a ledger – a huge database that is shared across the Bitcoin network just as ownership of a Rai stone was shared across the local memory. The database is transparent and there for all to see. Every bitcoin transaction that takes place for even the smallest amount – every detail is recorded on it. The database provides the mathematical evidence – the so-called 'crypto-proof' – on which Bitcoin is based.

It is called the 'block chain'.

## The evolution of digital cash - and the monies that failed

In 1955 and 1956, a generation of computer geniuses was born. This gamechanging cohort includes Tim Berners Lee, Bill Gates, Steve Jobs – and a little-known mathematician by the name of David Chaum.

Chaum was one of the pioneers of early cryptography and the grandfather of digital cash. He first proposed the idea of digital cash in 1982,[15] then developed his thinking in 1985 with the fantastically titled paper, *Security Without Identification: Transaction Systems to Make Big Brother Obsolete*. By the late 1980s he had teamed up with two Israeli cryptographers – Amos Fiat and Moni Naor – and they wrote the paper *Untraceable Electronic Cash*.

In 1990, Chaum founded the company Digicash to try to commercialize his ideas. This led to the development of 'ecash', which you could use to 'safely and anonymously pay over the Internet'.[16] At this moment in history, credit cards were still considered unsafe and insecure. It was not clear who was going to win the battle to control internet payments.

Company after company became interested in Digicash, but each time, Chaum scuppered the deal. He faxed a copy of one offer he received to all the other interested parties – and, in retaliation, the other parties pulled out. ING and Goldman Sachs were about to list Digicash on the stock market, but on the day of the deal – with eight VIPs from the two banks in the room – Chaum refused to sign. Bill Gates is said to have made an offer of $100 million, wanting to integrate ecash into every copy of Windows 95. But allegedly Chaum wanted two dollars per sold copy of Windows 95. In 1996, Visa wanted to invest $40 million – Chaum asked for 75.

Sometimes he wanted more money. Sometimes, say those who worked with him, he got paranoid. Sometimes he was too controlling. Throughout he believed so arrogantly in the superiority of his product that he thought a better offer was always just around the corner.

Eventually he paid the price for his hubris. He never made the deal – and credit cards won the battle to control electronic payment.

Chaum faded into the background and in 1999 Digicash went bust.

(By the way, if I'm correct in my assessment of who he is, Satoshi even worked for Digicash in the 1990s.)

Perhaps the most famous digital money before Bitcoin was E-gold.

E-gold was the invention of an oncologist and economic history buff, Douglas Jackson, and an attorney named Barry Downey.

The idea was that you could open an account, buy some gold and then use that gold as means of payment to other E-gold account holders.

E-gold was founded in 1996. By 1999 – even though gold itself was right at the bottom of a 20-year bear market – it was already so successful that the *Financial Times* called it 'the only electronic currency that has achieved critical mass on the web'.[17] Jackson believed his payment system, backed by solid gold, would eventually rival fiat currencies.

At its zenith in 2008, E-gold was processing over $2 billion worth of transactions a year with some four million accounts open. The problem was many of these accounts were operated by money-launderers and drug-dealers. It fell victim to hacking, fraud and identity theft. E-gold was already under FBI investigation in 2005. By 2009, it had been shut down.

Its founders faced all sorts of legal calamities – and are still dealing with the fall-out. I've no doubt seeing their fate is part of the reason Bitcoin's founder so prizes his anonymity.

Other companies with similar models to E-gold sprang up and failed in the Noughties – eBullion, Standard Reserve, INTGold and even a multi-million dollar Ponzi scheme that had no gold at all, OS-Gold. James Turk, founder of the gold storage facility Goldmoney, had also patented an e-gold payments system, but Goldmoney abandoned this in 2012 because of the cost of compliance.

So, Digicash failed because it had an erratic man in charge and it went bust. E-gold failed because the FBI shut it down.

For all their genius, the success of both systems was dependent on the companies that ran them – they had a central point of failure.

'A lot of people automatically dismiss e-currency as a lost cause because of all the companies that failed since the 1990s,' said Satoshi. 'I hope it's obvious it was only the centrally controlled nature of those systems that doomed them. I think this is the first time we're trying a decentralized, non-trust-based system.'[18]

Bitcoin is different. There is no single company that issues the coins or maintains the system. It is a distributed network – there is no central point of failure.

## How Bitcoin works

If I send you an email, I can, if I want, then copy and paste that email and send it to someone else. I could do the same with a picture, a document, a film – any form of digital code. What's to stop me doing the same with digital cash – cutting and pasting the code and spending the same piece of cash over and over again? This is the problem of double spending.

This is not, of course, a problem with physical cash. I cannot give the same dollar bill to two people at once. But it has been one of the fundamental problems of digital cash. If people can spend the same money twice, they'll find ways to spend it hundreds of times over, rendering the money useless.

Banks prevent this happening. Take old-fashioned cheques. If I wrote two cheques for $10 each and I only had $10 in my account, the bank would decide which one to honour and which one to bounce. With internet banking, they have other preventative systems in place.

PayPal, as blogger Gwern notes, processes transactions in real time, 'so you cannot log into your PayPal account in two different browsers and send your entire balance to two different people'.[19]

Both Digicash and E-gold also relied on a central body to log all transactions and police the network.

But all these systems, whether they use fiat money, gold or ecash, rely on a so-called 'trusted third party'. That was unacceptable to Satoshi.

'The usual solution is for a trusted company with a central database to check for double-spending', he says, 'but that just gets back to the trust model. In its central position, the company can override the users, and the fees needed to support the company make micropayments impractical...'[20]

But, in a distributed system without centralization, there is a different set of problems. Who runs it? Who has power of veto? With two conflicting transactions, who decides which is the real one? Who prevents double spending? Put another way, how do you guarantee trust?

This was something that had confounded computer scientists for years, so much so that the idea of digital cash had all but been abandoned. It was known as the Byzantine Generals problem.[21] And Satoshi solved it.

The solution lay in the block chain.

In ordinary life, neither you nor I can create money. We can earn it. We can be given it. But we can't create it out of nothing.

Bitcoin is different. If you want to, it is possible to make them yourself.

Obviously this is quite a startling idea. So let's go through it slowly.

You make bitcoins, or, to use the correct term, you 'mine' them by downloading the Bitcoin software and running it on your computer.

That's right. Anyone with a computer can, in theory, 'mine' bitcoins – just as, once upon a time, one could mine gold and silver, or collect shells or salt.

Early in Bitcoin's evolution, when few coins existed, an ordinary home computer was more than enough to mine coins. But, as bitcoins have grown in value, competition to mine them has grown – and, as a result, so has the amount of computer processing power required for mining. Now you need many powerful computers working in tandem consuming large amounts of electricity. Look up professional mining operations on YouTube and you'll see huge banks of computers all whirring endlessly away.

When you run the software – when you mine – what actually happens is that you maintain the block chain. You are adding and verifying the records of every recent transaction on the public ledger – compiling it all into a block. A block is, in effect, a file with a record of recent transactions, like a page in a book of accounts. Each new block is then added to the chain – thus you have the block chain. Once a block is added, it is never changed.

Imagine a record of every dollar transaction, however large or small, that has ever taken place and of every new dollar that has been created. It would be amazing and enormous. That is what the block chain is for Bitcoin – an astonishingly comprehensive and completely public record. It will continue to grow – but it needs a great deal of maintenance.

In exchange for mining a block, you are rewarded with bitcoins. So, the dynamic is that people are incentivized to maintain the block chain. It is in people's interests to mine coins – you're, effectively, printing your own money. Bitcoin makes use of this self-interest.

As well as a record of recent transactions and a reference to the block that came immediately before, each new block also contains the answer to a complex mathematical puzzle. There are now computers all over the world all competing to solve the puzzle – and thus mine the block – in order to receive the bitcoin reward.

The computer that solves the puzzle first mines the block. Then the race to mine the next block begins.

A block is mined every ten minutes. The network automatically adjusts the difficulty of the mathematical problem in order to maintain this average of six blocks per hour. If blocks are solved quickly, the puzzles become more complicated – and vice versa.

The idea also is that money should have a cost of production to it. Money should not be free (as it is at the moment for those lucky bodies, governments and banks, that have the ability to create it). Just as gold and silver cost money to mine – and there's no guarantee that in spending money on mining you'll actually find and produce metal – so do bitcoins. Bitcoin is a deliberate digital replication of the mining process. Early bitcoins were easy to mine – so is surface gold. As the mine goes deeper underground, it gets more expensive and labour intensive.

So, the cost of bitcoin production is block chain maintenance.

At present, you receive 25 bitcoins (current value about

$12,500) for successfully mining a block. The number of coins will fall as more blocks get mined. There are currently about 12 million bitcoins in existence. The eventual maximum will be 21 million – there is a finite supply.

When that maximum is reached, you will no longer be rewarded with new bitcoins when you mine – but mining will still be profitable. Instead, the reward for maintaining the block chain will come from small commissions paid by users every time they send coins.

Effectively, all these computers around the world are voluntarily competing to maintain the block chain and keep it secure. The system is self-reinforcing. The network of miners effectively becomes the public record keeper and regulator – like a decentralized central bank.

The mining process also serves another function – the dissemination of new coins. Different computers win each race to mine a block, so different computers add to the block chain and different people get the new bitcoins. The effect is one of distribution and decentralization.

One computer might conk out, a mining company might go bust, but another will still mine the next block – and the block chain, which is distributed across the network, is maintained. Without the block chain, Bitcoin is useless. Satoshi described 'a currency based on crypto-proof rather than trust',[22] the block chain provides that proof.

Protected by computation and a distributed network, rather than by the manufacturer, the decentralized block chain has enabled Bitcoin to succeed where others failed. The same fate that struck those other forms of digital cash does not await Bitcoin because it has no central point of failure. A government can make using Bitcoin illegal, the world can lose all interest and move on to something else, but the system cannot be shut down. How do you shut down something that is distributed? Nobody has yet found a way.

Here for the first time was a way to safely send a piece of digital property to someone else without the need for third party contracts and guarantees. Thanks to the block chain, everybody now knows the transfer has taken place, and nobody can challenge its legitimacy. Blogger Gwern writes: 'The underappreciated genius of Bitcoin is that it says that the valid transaction is simply "the one which had the most computing power invested in producing it"...Within hours, one transaction will be universal, and the other forgotten'.[23]

First we had money backed by things, and then we had money backed by political command; now we have money backed by mathematical proof.

What's more, the core technology has so far proved unhackable.

## The most reliable and secure digital technology ever invented

Dan Kaminsky is an internet security researcher, famous among hackers 'for discovering, in 2008, a fundamental flaw in the Internet which would have allowed a skilled coder to take over any website or even to shut down the Internet'.[24]

'When I first looked at the (Bitcoin) code', he says, 'I was sure I was going to be able to break it. The way the whole thing was formatted was insane. Only the most paranoid, painstaking coder in the world could avoid making mistakes.'

He devised 15 bugs he thought he could use to hack it.

Every time he would get a response along the lines of 'Attack Removed'.

'I came up with beautiful bugs', he said. 'But every time I went after the code there was a line that addressed the problem. I've never seen anything like it...Either there's a team of people who worked on this or this guy is a genius.'[25]

Kaminsky continued, 'Here was a system (that)...Created an enormous global cloud of always-on, listening machine; Spoke its own fiddly little custom network protocol; (is) Written in C++, which for all of its strengths is not usually the safest thing in the world to be reading random internet garbage with; (and) Directly implemented the delivery of a Pot Of Gold At The End Of The Rainbow for any hacker who could break it. By all extant metrics in security system review, this system should have failed instantaneously, at every possible layer...But the core technology actually works...my fifteen point list of obvious likely bugs was systematically destroyed by a codebase that quite frankly knew better.'[26]

What was exceptional was the robustness of Bitcoin. The pitfalls and security problems that even experienced programmers usually end up accidentally creating in their code were almost completely absent. The implication was that Satoshi, coding skills aside, had a great deal of theoretical and practical know-how. He was savvy. Alessandro Polverini, an Italian coder, tells me in an email, 'My guess is that Satoshi is not a professional developer but a very highly skilled hacker, probably working in the security field.'

In fact, the protocol is so bulletproof that it has led some experts to believe a government agency created it.

You've heard about bankruptcies, hackings, thefts and

fraud, for example. This is because companies using the protocol – certain exchanges, for example (so-called third parties) – have not acted like proper financial institutions. Certain operating systems using the protocol are insecure, rendering bitcoins vulnerable to theft. There are also issues with programmers who have failed to understand the block chain. But while the edges of Bitcoin are vulnerable, the core protocol is sound.

The simple fact that it works is what has enabled Bitcoin to take off in the way that it has. It's also what enabled Satoshi to be so modest in his promotion of it. Blogger Mike Hearn writes: 'It cannot be understated: the Bitcoin protocol is a monumental technological achievement. Regardless of whether the system will prove to be a real-world alternative to fiat currency, the technical achievement is undeniable. It solves several previously unsolved cryptographic problems surrounding "distributed trust" (for example, the Byzantine Generals' Problem) and synthesizes technologies such as public-key cryptography, proof-of-work systems (using SHA-256), peer-to-peer and others.'

Nick Szabo, a computer scientist believed by many to be Satoshi, and inventor of a precursor to Bitcoin called bit gold, wrote in an email to me, 'The core protocol of Bitcoin is sound, and has an unprecedented reliability and security. In other words the core technology is more reliable and secure than any other digital technology that has ever been fielded.' That is some achievement.

Some hackers see Bitcoin's creation as a seminal point in the history of information technology. Rather as we have BC and AD, they have proposed that before 3 January 2009 (the date of the Genesis Block) be named Before Satoshi (BS) and after Bitcoin Era (BE).

That's a lovely idea – though perhaps BN (Before Nakamoto) is preferable to BS.

Well done. You've just finished the hardest chapter in the book.

# 2

# THE ANARCHIC COMPUTING SUBCULTURE IN WHICH BITCOIN HAS ITS ROOTS

*Cypherpunks write code.*

— Eric Hughes, mathematician and Cypherpunk

In September 1992, Tim May, a computer scientist whose inventions had once made him a great deal of money at Intel, invited a group of eminent, free-thinking programmers to his house in Santa Cruz, California, near Silicon Valley. They were there to discuss this exciting new development called the internet. They were excited about the possibilities, but they were also concerned. Privacy was their issue.

Beyond the realm of cash payments, no transaction is private. And your financial behaviour says more about you than anything. Banks, credit card companies, merchants and – most worryingly for Tim May and his friends – the government would all have access to this information on the internet. How would they use it? They were scared of Big Brother.

Some of the group simply wanted to find ways to protect privacy, others wanted to fight back. Their mistrust was born of experience. Their friend, the programmer Phil Zimmerman, was under criminal investigation for a simple piece of privacy software he had developed called PGP (Pretty Good Privacy). He was in serious trouble with the US authorities, who said he had violated the Arms Export Control Act.

'Just as the technology of printing altered and reduced the power of medieval guilds and the social power structure', said May that night, 'so too will cryptologic methods fundamentally alter the nature of corporations and of government interference in economic transactions...just as a seemingly minor invention like barbed wire made possible the fencing-off of vast ranches and farms, thus altering forever the concepts of land and property rights in the frontier West, so too will the seemingly minor discovery out of an arcane branch of mathematics come to be the wire clippers which dismantle the barbed wire around intellectual property. Arise, you have nothing to lose but your barbed wire fences!' [27]

They were a committed, disparate and talented group of computer scientists. Their belief system was largely libertarian; they understood the potential of the internet, but they also saw the possibilities it was opening up for state and corporate invasion of privacy. They thought cryptography could lead to social and political change. By the end of the meeting, an anarchist philosophy had been born, that of the Cypherpunks.

Within a week mathematician Eric Hughes, a co-founder of the movement, had written a programme that could receive encrypted emails, remove any signs by which they could be identified and send them out to a list of subscribers. Now they had the Cypherpunks Mailing List. On this email list, they would share, discuss and develop their ideas.

When you signed up, you were greeted with a message from Hughes: 'Cypherpunks assume privacy is a good thing and wish there were more of it. Cypherpunks acknowledge that those who want privacy must create it for themselves and not expect governments, corporations, or other large, faceless organizations to grant them privacy out of beneficence'.

That message became the spine of his *Cypherpunk Manifesto*.[28]

Privacy is the power to selectively reveal oneself to the world. When I purchase a magazine at a store and hand cash to the clerk, there is no need to know who I am. When I ask my electronic mail provider to send and receive messages, my provider need not know to whom I am speaking or what I am saying...my provider only need know how to get the message there and how much I owe them in fees. When my identity is revealed by the underlying mechanism of the transaction, I have no privacy. I cannot here selectively reveal myself; I must always reveal myself...If I say something, I want it heard only by those for whom I intend it...We must defend our own privacy if we expect to have any. We must come together and create systems which allow anonymous transactions to take place...Cypherpunks are therefore devoted to cryptography. Cypherpunks wish to learn about it, to teach it, to implement it, and to make more of it...We the Cypherpunks are dedicated to building anonymous systems. We are defending our privacy with cryptography, with anonymous mail forwarding systems, with digital signatures, and with electronic money...Our code is free for all to use, worldwide. The Cypherpunks are actively engaged in making the networks safer for privacy. Let us proceed together apace.[29]

Their mantra, 'Cypherpunks write code', meant that rather than talk about how things should be, they would make things as they should be through computer code. If a system isn't working, write some code and make it work.

The ultimate dream of the movement was a system of digital cash outside the invasive capabilities of governments or banks. Many attempts have since been made. Each one failed.

Until Bitcoin: the realization of the Cypherpunk dream.

# The Cypherpunks on whose shoulders Bitcoin is standing

We all know about spam. It's extremely annoying. Worse, it's often dangerous. There is the risk of viruses, worms, Trojans, spyware and adware. Your identity can get stolen; your bank account hacked.

If there's one thing a Cypherpunk hates more than an

intrusive government, it is spam – and all the invasions of privacy that come with it.

In 1997, a young English Cypherpunk, a programmer named Adam Back, proposed a system to limit email spam and denial-of-service attacks. (DoS attacks are attempts, usually by hackers, to make a computer or a network unusable.)

Like many good ideas, the principle behind Back's idea was simple. And, as he wryly noted to me, several others have since had the 'same' idea.

He would make spam uneconomic.

Spam is predicated on being able to send large numbers of emails at low cost. But if each individual email involves effort and cost, then the spam becomes uneconomic – and so less likely to happen. Back's idea was that emails should contain evidence that some kind of effort had gone into their composition – a proof of work. An email that contains proof of work is an email that is less likely to contain spam.

He developed a system called 'Hashcash'. This added a textual stamp to the header of an email. It was proof that the sender had expended a certain amount of time in writing and sending the email.

In 2004, another computer programmer, Hal Finney, built on Back's proof-of-work system.

Finney's idea was that each proof of work could be re-used, so that the work that went into them would not have to be repeated. He called it 'reusable proof of work' (RPOW). If a Hashcash stamp could become a token denoting a certain amount of work, it would have some kind of value. In other words, Hashcash stamps could work as a form of digital money.

Finney was highly regarded in the computer programming world, but his system never saw any economic use.

Until Bitcoin.

All a bitcoin is, essentially, is a re-usable proof of work. As Back says, 'bitcoin mining is basically my hashcash invention' – with a few small technical adaptations.

But, of course, there's more to it than that.

In November 1998, shortly after Back's Hashcash proposal, another coder by the name of Wei Dai proposed his idea 'b-money'.

He also suggested using Hashcash stamps as money. His proposal was that, as money is transferred, the transaction would be broadcast to all parties on the money network, who can then keep account. There is a public ledger in other words – a type of block chain.

Satoshi actually cites Dai in his original white paper, as he did Back, but it's not clear how much influence Dai actually had.[30] Just as Back wasn't the only person to come up with the proof of work idea, Dai wasn't the only person to conceive of a public ledger.

At around the same time as Wei Dai, Nick Szabo, another computer scientist, proposed his idea – bit gold.[31]

If bit gold sounds eerily similar to Bitcoin, that's because it is.

Both are based around chains of proofs of work.

'I started thinking about the analogy between difficult-to-solve problems and the difficulty of mining gold,' Szabo says.[32]

If something took effort to solve, then it could have value. With bit gold, computer power would be used to solve mathematical puzzles or equations. The solved equations would be sent to the community. If accepted, the person (or computer) that had solved the puzzle would receive a credit, a gold bit. Their solution would become part of the next puzzle. This meant the network would have to verify and stamp new bits otherwise they couldn't start on the next puzzle.

'I was trying to mimic as closely as possible in cyberspace the security and trust characteristics of gold', he continues, 'and chief among those is that it doesn't depend on a trusted central authority'.[33]

As well as having a cost of production, bit gold's public acceptance of solved puzzles – that the network must approve them – would obviate the need for a central authority.

There are a few small technical differences, but the similarities between Szabo's bit gold and Bitcoin are uncanny. But Satoshi was the one who actually coded his idea and put it into practice.

Back, Finney, Dai and Szabo were all Cypherpunks. Bitcoin has implemented all of their ideas, and the ideas of many more besides.[34] Without these developments, Bitcoin almost certainly could not have happened. It was 'standing on the shoulders of Cypherpunks', to misquote Isaac Newton – who, incidentally, also laid down a new system of money: the gold standard on which Britain would thrive in the 18th and 19th centuries.

## Bitcoin's first year

It was two days before anyone even acknowledged Satoshi's creation.

'Announcing the first release of Bitcoin', he said. 'A new electronic cash system.'[35]

Nobody seemed to care.

Eventually a reply came from Hal Finney.

'Congratulations to Satoshi on this first alpha release,' he said. 'I am looking forward to trying it out...The possibility of generating coins today with a few cents of compute time may be quite a good bet, with a payoff of something like 100 million to 1! Even if the odds of Bitcoin succeeding to this degree are slim, are they really 100 million to one against? Something to think about.'[36]

'I would be surprised if 10 years from now we're not using electronic currency in some way, now that we know a way to do it', came the reply from Satoshi. 'It might make sense just to get some in case it catches on.'

How right he was.

They were talking on the Cryptography Mailing List – where the more technically minded Cypherpunks had gravitated when the Cypherpunks Mailing List closed down several years earlier in a flood of spam and squabbling.

On February 11th 2009, a month later, Satoshi would announce his e-cash system on the Peer-to-Peer Foundation forum, saying: 'I've developed a new open source P2P ecash system called Bitcoin. It's completely decentralized, with no central server or trusted parties, because everything is based on crypto proof instead of trust. Give it a try, or take a look at the screenshots and design paper.'[37]

In making this post, he would leave a tiny clue as to his identity. In his original Bitcoin white paper, in his posts on the Cryptography Mailing List and later on the BitcoinTalk forums, he used two spaces after a full stop. But here on the P2P Foundation, he used only one.

A short discussion followed his post that lasted a few days, then – online at least – it all went quiet.

In May 2009, a 20-year-old computer sciences student from Finland was searching to see if, he tells me, 'any peer-to-peer currencies had been successfully implemented'. Bitcoin was the only one he could find that didn't have centralized parties. This student was Martti Malmi, aka Sirius, the second developer to work on Bitcoin. The domain name bitcoin.org would eventually pass to him.

'If you googled, "Bitcoin",' he tells me, 'you'd find ten results or less. The paper had only been published a few months earlier. I emailed Satoshi and offered him help with the project. I liked the ideology, the interesting technology, the individual freedom – making money was not my motivation.

'I think Satoshi was taking a couple of months break from development and during that time I learnt C++, a computer code, the language Bitcoin was written in. I think Satoshi and I were the only developers until 2010 maybe. There may have been a third one. I am not quite sure...Bitcoin was already quite finished and operational when I joined the project. I didn't do anything to complicate it. I did some coding work to Linux (it was originally Windows only) and made some user interface improvements, and project organization – like websites, forums, teaching and advertising. But I don't want to take too much credit for what I did. Maybe I can give myself credit for, you know, understanding the system and believing at the time when people were just joking about it and wouldn't take it seriously. I realized the potential of this kind of monetary system, the theoretical possibility that it could change the future of money, but I was wondering why no one has done that before.'

While Satoshi and Sirius got to work, several more months passed. But in the open source movement, among programmers and on forums, Bitcoin was slowly starting to be talked about.

In February 2010 the first Bitcoin exchange – the Bitcoin Market – began trading. You could now buy bitcoins using PayPal.

In May 2010, a Florida programmer by the name of Laszlo Hanyecz wanted to test the technology. He offered to buy a pizza for 10,000 coins. The pizza arrived. For several days after that, Hanyecz bought 10,000-bitcoin pizzas. I bet he regrets it now. Ten thousand bitcoins would at one stage be worth over 12 million dollars. Twelve million bucks for a pizza!

July 2010 saw Bitcoin's first step out of obscurity. It was mentioned on the website Slashdot and there was a sudden increase in interest. The value of a bitcoin went up over ten times in a week – from eight-tenths of one cent to eight cents. The price would slide back to six cents and remain there for several months.

Then another Bitcoin exchange sprung up, one that would become the biggest and most notorious – MtGox.

# 3

# THE RISE OF BITCOIN AND THE DISAPPEARANCE OF ITS MAKER

*I think that the internet is going to be one of the major forces for reducing the role of government. The one thing that's missing, but that will soon be developed, is a reliable e-cash.*

— Milton Friedman, economist

The US Department of Defense called it the 'largest leak of classified documents in its history'.

It's difficult to overstate how big a threat to the existing world order WikiLeaks was perceived to be in late 2010. There has been revelation after revelation – the Bradley Manning leaks, the video of US soldiers shooting at Reuters cameramen, the 'friendly fire' and civilian casualties, then the leak of another 400,000 documents relating to the Iraq war.

WikiLeaks had caught the imagination of those opposed to the US and other governments. Many wanted to help.

PayPal was the main means by which WikiLeaks was able to receive funds for its activities and, in 2010, its donors gave around one million dollars. But on December 4th 2010, under pressure from the US government, PayPal froze the WikiLeaks account. Domain name providers and other payment systems followed suit and refused to handle WikiLeaks' business.

Julian Assange, the WikiLeaks boss, was involved in expensive litigation at the same time. WikiLeaks was starved of funds. And, unbeknownst to most, the organization was crumbling from within due to a falling-out between Daniel Domscheit-Berg, WikiLeaks' number two, and Assange.

One poster at BitcoinTalk thought that Bitcoin would be a means to help WikiLeaks. Others jumped at the idea. 'Bring it on,' said one. 'Let's encourage WikiLeaks to use Bitcoins and I'm willing to face any risk or fallout from that fact.'

Then wiser heads stepped in and a long discussion ensued.[38] Early developers such as Jeff Garzik, Bruce Wagner and others felt that the last thing they should do was bring the attention of authorities to Bitcoin this early in its evolution.

'It could permanently marginalize Bitcoin, keeping it out of the mainstream for good. Is that really the end result the Bitcoin community most desires? Does it make sense to actively give *multiple world governments* incentive to shut down Bitcoin?' asked Garzik. 'WikiLeaks is the enemy of major world powers right now, with many influential elites feeling that Assange committed an act of war against the United States, or, at a minimum, irrevocably disrupted world affairs. This is not some mailing list discussion or theoretical exercise; there are very real, very powerful organizations actively targeting WikiLeaks' network infrastructure, organizational infrastructure, and most importantly, financial infrastructure. It is extraordinarily unwise to make Bitcoin such a highly visible target, at such an early stage in this project. There could be a lot of "collateral damage" in the Bitcoin community while you make your principled stand.'

Even Satoshi, usually so understated in his opinions if they didn't relate to coding, said 'No, don't "bring it on". The project needs to grow gradually so the software can be strengthened along the way. I make this appeal to WikiLeaks not to try to use Bitcoin. Bitcoin is a small beta community in its infancy. You would not stand to get more than pocket change, and the heat you would bring would likely destroy us at this stage.'

Five days later *PC World* magazine published an article – *Could the WikiLeaks Scandal Lead to New Virtual Currency?*[39] It was the most prominent site yet to mention Bitcoin and suggested it may be the answer to WikiLeaks' funding problems. A sudden flood of traffic overwhelmed Bitcoin's website and it went down. When it came back up again, Satoshi wrote, 'It would have been nice to get this attention in any other context. WikiLeaks has kicked the hornet's nest, and the swarm is headed towards us.' Then Bitcoin was mentioned on Slashdot again, alongside WikiLeaks and the outspoken libertarian US congressman, Ron Paul.

Meanwhile, the Financial Action Task Force issued warnings that digital currencies were being used to finance terrorist groups.[40]

The following morning, on December 12th 2010, Satoshi outlined some technical developments he had made. 'I'm doing a quick build of what I have so far in case it's needed, before venturing into more complex ideas,'[41] he said.

That was the last public remark he would ever make.

He exchanged emails with certain Bitcoin developers for some months after that, before disappearing altogether. In one final email to co-developer Mike Hearn, who asked if he had retired permanently, Satoshi said he had 'moved on to other things.'

Gavin Andresen, another of the early developers, was perhaps the closest to Satoshi. In September 2011 he said, 'I haven't had email from Satoshi in a couple months actually. The last email I sent him I actually told him I was going to talk at the CIA. So it's possible that...that may have had something to with his deciding.'[42]

It's easy to assume that Satoshi was fearful of government authorities. He saw what was happening to Assange and to Bradley Manning, and what had befallen the founders of other forms of ecash. It's unlikely he wanted accusations of terrorism levelled against him. Even if they were unfounded, they could have ruined his life and the lives of those close to him. Whether it was WikiLeaks, the CIA or both that caused it, Satoshi had vanished.

# The rise of Bitcoin

That July 2010 mention on Slashdot was a catalyst. More and more users flocked to Bitcoin over the following months. New operations sprung up to mine coins. Open-source development of the protocol continued.

At first, the price of a bitcoin remained flat at around six cents, but then it began to rise. In November, it touched

50 cents. The market cap of Bitcoin passed the one-million-dollar mark.

Across the net a growing number of people were developing the technology and ways to apply it. An escrow transaction took place, then an over-the-counter (OTC) transaction (securities traded in some context other than on a formal exchange are OTC). There was the first payment from mobile phone to mobile phone, a short sale, then a call option (a bet on the price to rise). In the fast-developing spirit of crypto coin humour, three 100 trillion Zimbabwe dollar notes were traded for four bitcoins each. A put option (a bet on the price to fall) was written and sold.

By February 2011, 5.25 million bitcoins – a quarter of the eventual total Bitcoin supply – had been mined. The price had reached parity with the US dollar. There was more publicity at Slashdot and Hacker News, and a buzz on Twitter. The Bitcoin website was struggling to cope with the new traffic. And a new website had opened up by which you could buy and sell drugs, using Bitcoin as a means of payment – the Silk Road.

As is often the case when a security gets a surge in publicity, Bitcoin reached a fleeting high. The following month its price fell 30%, but its international reach was growing. Markets for exchanging bitcoins opened up in the UK, Brazil and Poland.

In April 2011, Jerry Brito wrote in *Time*, 'If it catches on, Bitcoin might pose a threat not just to governments, but to payment processors as well. And it's a story that's just getting started'.[43] Bitcoin soon reached parity with the US dollar again, then the euro, then the pound. Its market cap exceeded ten million dollars. The two-and-a-half-month period from April to June 2011 saw spectacular gains. From an early April low of 60 cents the price rose to $32 in June. By November it had fallen to two dollars.

The criminals and hackers also moved in. A user by the name of Allinvain says he had 25,000 bitcoins (with a then equivalent value of US$375,000) stolen from his wallet. Some 600 account-holders at MyBitcoin had their balances stolen. Someone hacked into the administrator account of the bitcoin exchange MtGox and issued sell orders for hundreds of thousands of fake bitcoins, driving the price down from $17.50 to $0.01, albeit temporarily. Fraud concerning PayPal purchases of bitcoins meant that service was discontinued (although the connection with WikiLeaks may have been the real reason). The world's third largest exchange, Bitomat in Poland, lost its wallet and, with it, 17,000 bitcoins they were holding for clients. The wallet had been stored with Amazon's cloud computing servers and just 'disappeared'.

New developments continued to spring up – a smartphone wallet, then an iPad app. A payment was made by near field communication – a form of radio communication between smart phones. The first decentralized mining pool, P2Pool, mined a block. August saw the first Bitcoin conference in the US, and the following November Europe had its first conference in Prague.

Overall, 2012 was a year of consolidation, development and relative quiet for Bitcoin. Its volatile price pattern – one of huge, quick gains, followed by long, drawn-out declines – continued. It more than tripled between November 2011 and January 2012 – then it halved again. The price now stood at $4. In late May 2012, a bullish trend drove the coins from $5 to $17, only for the price to fall to $7. There was another six-month period of flat trading, this time in the $12 range which ended in January 2013.

There was further technological progress and increased media coverage. New companies sprung up offering everything from mining hardware to Bitcoin debit cards to Bitcoin gambling.

In May, it was discovered that the FBI were following developments. According to a leaked report,[44] they were worried about Bitcoin facilitating the sale of weapons and drugs (which it was doing).

The thefts continued. In March 2012 the largest theft of bitcoins to date would take place with over 46,000 stolen at the website hosting company Linode. Two more thefts in May and September took another 42,000 in total.

Despite these problems, Bitcoin moved further into the mainstream.

WordPress is the world's most popular blogging system. It powers about one in every six websites in the world,[45] including the likes of *The New York Times*, CNN, Reuters, General Motors, UPS, eBay, Sony and Volkswagen. On November 15th 2012, in order to open up WordPress to users in countries not supported by PayPal or other credit card companies, WordPress began accepting bitcoins.

## 2013: Bitcoin's year

2013 would be the year of Bitcoin. From low to high, it rose over 100 times. The old June 2011 high of $32 was utterly shattered by February. By March, the market cap of Bitcoin now exceeded one billion dollars. And for a day in November, a bitcoin would be worth the same price as an ounce of gold.

But back in January, the island nation of Cyprus was in economic crisis.

The EU then announced bail-ins – anyone with deposits above €100,000 would have a percentage of their money taken (47.5% as it eventually turned out) in order to raise funds for the over-leveraged Cypriot banks. Fears that these bail-ins would become the template for banks elsewhere spread across an extremely jittery Europe. Money – a lot of it Russian – fled European banks and Bitcoin became a vehicle to escape capital controls, pushing its price north of $100 in March. At the climax of the panic, it hit $266, only to collapse to $70 a week later. Over the next six months, the range was flat around $100.

More organizations started accepting bitcoins. Venture capital began pouring into the sector, despite continuing criminal activity ranging from hacking to money laundering.

One notorious organization – the Texas Bitcoin Savings and Trust – was accused of being a Ponzi scheme. In court, its founder Trendon Shavers tried to argue that bitcoins are not real money to sidestep misappropriation-of-funds charges, but the judge ruled that 'Bitcoin is a currency or form of money.' In August, Bitcoin was also ruled a unit of account by the German Federal Ministry of Finance.

In October, after some three years of trying, the FBI finally managed to shut down the Silk Road and seized some 27,000 bitcoins. The expectation was that the bitcoin price would collapse – and that day it fell by about 30%. On the same day, the Bitcoin forums were hacked and users' details stolen. Visitors to the site were greeted with cartoon images of missiles exploding as Tchaikovsky's 1812 Overture played in the background.

But the price immediately turned and set off a run that would take it to parity with gold.

One sub-corporation of China's answer to Google – Baidu – started accepting bitcoins as payment. It seemed the Chinese were now speculating. The price broke to new highs above $263 per coin. A fortnight later, it had doubled again. There was a hearing in the US Senate entitled 'Beyond Silk Road: Potential Risks, Threats and Promises of Virtual Currencies'. The next day the price doubled again, reaching an all-time high of $1,242. Bitcoin transaction volume was now exceeding that of Western Union Money Transfer.

It may have been Chinese speculation that drove the price up. It may also have been an enormous fraud at MtGox – as has recently been suggested.[46] It is not yet known for sure.

The University of Nicosia in Cyprus began accepting bitcoins as payment for tuition – suggesting a connection between Cypriot bail-ins and Bitcoin's price rise. Richard Branson's Virgin Galactic followed suit, then the ecommerce site Shopify.

December 2013 saw a heist at another online black market – Sheep Market Place. Another blow followed. China's central bank banned financial institutions from using Bitcoin. The price dropped 20%. Baidu stopped accepting bitcoins the next day. Ten days later, China banned Bitcoin transactions altogether.

Bitcoin's dark period continued into 2014.

Russian authorities said, 'Systems for anonymous payments and cyber currencies that have gained considerable circulation – including the most well-known, Bitcoin – are money substitutes and cannot be used by individuals or legal entities.'[47] Russian law, they said, stipulated that the rouble was the sole official currency and that introducing any other monetary units or substitutes was illegal. Remember, post-Cyprus, a lot of Russian money came in to Bitcoin.

Meanwhile people were struggling to withdraw their money from the world's largest Bitcoin exchange. MtGox was going under.

## Being in the right place at the right time isn't everything - the ignominious rise and fall of MtGox

MtGox was the world's largest and best-known Bitcoin exchange.

It was originally founded in 2007 by Jed McCaleb – who *Wired* described rather disparagingly as 'an unemployed computer hacker' – as an exchange for the trading cards game 'Magic: The Gathering'. Hence the weird name – MtGox is an acronym of 'Magic The Gathering Online eXchange'. (It is not pronounced Mount Gox – but 'em-tee-gox' – as in 'empty promises', as someone wryly put it.) Initially, the site was only used for a few months.

In July 2010, McCaleb saw that seminal post about Bitcoin on the website Slashdot – the mention that would draw attention to Bitcoin to an audience beyond the handful of programmers developing the code at the time. McCaleb thought it looked like a good idea, and quickly turned the MtGox domain name he had lying around into an exchange for bitcoins.

The site became *the* portal for buying and selling bitcoins. But McCaleb lost interest and in March 2011 sold MtGox to the Japanese company Tibanne, run by Mark Karpelès.

By April 2012 it was handling some 70% of global Bitcoin trades. But, despite MtGox riding on the coat tails of the stratospheric rise of Bitcoin, it had always been dogged with problems – hacks, thefts, lawsuits, and clients complaining they couldn't retrieve funds. In the spring of 2013, US regulators declared that Bitcoin exchanges had to comply with money-laundering laws. MtGox failed to do so and had three million dollars seized by the Department of Homeland Security.

In 2014, withdrawals were halted again, then started, and then halted. At one stage, so weak was trust in the exchange that the MtGox quoted bitcoin price was about a quarter of that elsewhere. People flew to Japan to demonstrate outside MtGox's offices and try to get their money back. An extremely wealthy tech-millionaire told me that Karpelès had been on the phone to him asking for financial help.

On February 24th, Karpelès resigned from the Bitcoin Foundation. The following day the MtGox website was taken down, its Twitter feed was deleted, withdrawals were frozen and a rumour began circulating that some 744,408 bitcoins – over 350 million dollars' worth – had been stolen. All you got when you visited the MtGox site was a blank screen. The next day there was a message that read:

Dear MtGox Customers,

In light of recent news reports and the potential repercussions on MtGox's operations and the market, a decision was taken to close all transactions for the time being in order to protect the site and our users.

We will be closely monitoring the situation and will react accordingly.

Best regards,

*MtGox Team*

The following day another statement was issued:

February 26th 2014

Dear MtGox Customers,

As there is a lot of speculation regarding MtGox and its future, I would like to use this opportunity to reassure everyone that I am still in Japan, and working very hard with the support of different parties to find a solution to our recent issues.

Furthermore I would like to kindly ask that people refrain from asking questions to our staff: they have been instructed not to give any response or information. Please visit this page for further announcements and updates.

Sincerely,

Mark Karpelès

Other exchanges were quick to distance themselves, declaring that the 'tragic violation of the trust of users of MtGox was the result of one company's actions and does not reflect the resilience or value of Bitcoin and the digital currency industry'. But many people had lost fortunes.

The BBC's Robert Peston called it, a little hysterically, 'Bitcoin's life-or-death moment.'[48] James Titcomb in the *Tele-*

*graph* said, 'Bitcoin is under threat.'[49] But this was not the failure of Bitcoin, it was the failure of one badly run company operating on the Bitcoin protocol.

I came across this post on Reddit by 'mtreme':

I want to start off by saying that I've been waiting for this moment for a while. I knew it was bound to happen sooner or later, as soon as we weren't able to withdraw our coins from Mt. Gox weeks ago. I stupidly had my life's savings in bitcoin, and when the price started to fall, I converted to dollars and watched the price plummet. I lost $357,000. Not to try to earn a bunch of sympathy or anything but this was not only my money but it was going to be my 5 year old son's education fund which i took out of fidelity about 1 year ago to mess with bitcoins. I dont know what the fuck to do any more. I'm sitting here on reddit looking for comfort or just something but I don't know what I'm going to do now at all. I don't have shit to live for any more and the only thing I have left is just talking about it here I guess. I can't express what I'm feeling right now. THat shit was just sitting there and I couldn't take it out how could this whole shop just pack up and dissapear? I don't know if anyone here knows the facts or whats going on but I want to or if you have any slighest shred of evidence that its possible they arent really gone please et me know here. if im never going to see my money again all of it im going to either kill myself which i dont want to do because i want to live even though i have nothing to live for now, except my son who is now completely fucked[50]

Many positive messages of support followed.

'Your son is not fucked, he still has his father. Hang on' said one. 'Kids tend to love fathers more than money. Stay positive, dude' said another. 'Sir, I would give anything, 357k, a million, every cent I've ever earned or will earn to have one more day with my dad. Be there for your son' said a third.

That sad post articulates the misery many feel when they lose money gambling, speculating or investing. (I suspect that – as well as the opposite extreme emotion you feel at winning – is part of the reason so many professional speculators from Jesse Livermore to the present day have been manic-depressives.)

This kind of disaster is also rude capitalism at work. MtGox was badly run. It was at best out of its depth, and at worst a scam. If the rumours are true, how can anybody run a company and not notice 350 million dollars' worth of its core product disappearing? My sympathies are with those who have lost money, very much so. But these kinds of losses will, hopefully, force participants in the future to act better.

If Bitcoin is to succeed, it needs good practice from companies operating in the sector. Failure – bad companies going under – is how you achieve that.

Other exchanges quickly appear to have improved their act as a result. Vault of Satoshi (not a company I am endorsing) is one example. Its manager, Adam Cochran, announced, not long after the bust of MtGox, that third-party audits were not enough: 'At Vault of Satoshi we are proud to announce full proof of solvency and the publication of our cold wallet.' (A cold wallet is a bitcoin wallet kept offline.) 'Users can self validate both their balance and the overall reserves of the exchange by navigating to our security center and selecting "BTC Proof of Solvency".'[51]

Herein, by the way, lies one of the problems with Bitcoin. As a form of cash, it has the problem that it is non-reversible. There's no form of payment protection. That's great for merchants, but risky for customers. How do you get your money back, if the merchant doesn't want to give it to you? Escrow and other forms of payment protection can be built on Bitcoin – but then you're back to third parties with all the associated costs and need for trust.

Such forms of protection are already being developed. Whether you choose them or not is up to you.

Meanwhile, as I write, MtGox is in legal proceedings.

# 4

# NERDS, SQUATS AND MILLIONAIRES

*I do think Bitcoin...has the potential to do something like change the world.*

— Peter Thiel, Co-Founder of PayPal

It is January 2014.

'Informal Bitcoin get-together,' says the link I've been texted. 'Saturday 1pm to 4pm. Meet under the blue awning at St James Square in Spitalfields.'

I arrive about 1.45. There is no blue awning. But a group of 70 people are milling under a white one. It's bitterly cold.

'Ask me,' says a sticker on the coat of a young chap with a bowler hat. So I do. Yes, this is the Bitcoin get-together.

He's a computer programmer for a financial services company. Late twenties I'd guess. He's been into bitcoins for a while. Thinks the price has got ahead of itself. But he's still into it. We start talking about the future of Bitcoin; whether it's going to change the world, that kind of thing.

A dude with a gold tooth and a blue leather jacket starts listening in.

'You got any bitcoins, then?' he asks after a while.

'A couple,' I say.

'How did you get them?'

'I was given them a while back.'

'Ah.'

He thinks for a moment.

'But have you ever actually used them?' he asks.

'Yeah. Once or twice. I bought weed on the Silk Road.'

'What's that? I've heard of that, I think.'

'It's a website where you could buy drugs and stuff – using bitcoins.'

'What and it actually arrived?'

'Yeah. A couple of days after I ordered it. From "Mr Clonk".'

'Wow!' he says thoughtfully. I can see all sorts of ideas going through his head.

Next, I meet a middle-class white kid with tatty clothes and a confident air. He's developing a system by which you can buy and sell goods on Amazon with bitcoins. He's hoping to close the deal with Amazon next week.

Then I meet Fabio, an Italian computer programmer who wants to convert his brother's pizza delivery company in Dubai to bitcoin only. Then there's an Eastern European whose name I didn't catch who bought bitcoins because Max Keiser told him to. He bought gold because of Max – that hasn't worked out – but he believes in what Keiser is saying, so he bought bitcoins too. They've done better.

Then I meet Seshu from Bangalore who's developing a bitcoin bank, which pays 80% interest. Yes, 80%. It also provides means by which people can make leveraged bets in bitcoins.

'In my PR, when I talk about "leverage" and "gearing", do you think people will understand what that means?' he asks, concerned.

This all happens in about 15 minutes. I'm amazed at the creativity Bitcoin is inspiring and the opportunities it is creating.

A chubby posh chap in an oilskin coat stands on a table.

'All right, we're going to have a live auction. Could everybody gather round? The people who are selling over here. The people who are buying over here. So what am I offered?'

'Five hundred and thirty pounds,' comes a call. 'Five thirty for one bitcoin.'

'Five fifteen,' comes an offer from a bloke with a beard who looks like Captain Birdseye.

'Five twenty-five,' suggests the seller.

'Meet there?' ventures our auctioneer.

After a moment, they both nod.

'Sold. We have our first sale of the afternoon. Right, five twenty-five is the price. Do we have any more?'

He's clearly done this before – and is a natural.

Over the course of the next few minutes I watch as several bitcoins change hands. Wads of notes are passed and bitcoins are transferred via mobile phone or computer.

A friend and I once got involved in a pyramid scheme in the late 1990s. You paid £3,000 to get your place on the pyramid. You then, if I remember right, had to find eight people beneath you each paying £3,000 to you, so you made £24,000. They then had to find eight more. Did I make money? Er, no. This scene reminded me of the meetings I went to then, with large wads of cash being passed about. It's a pyramid scheme, a Ponzi scheme, a scam. Alarm bells are going off. Should I get rid of my coins here and now?

Now, like then, there are all sorts at the meeting. In addition to those already mentioned there are several Indians, a load of black guys either African or London-born, a proper Shoreditch twit with ridiculous hair and white leather jacket, people from all over Europe, a load of grungy-looking guys who are either homeless (complete with tracksuits, hoodies, roll ups, cans of lager and rotten teeth) or perennials on the festival circuit, a few couples, some city bods of various shapes and sizes, and goodness knows what else. Heck, there's even a transvestite. I've never seen so much variety in 70 people – except for the fact that 90% are blokes. Some are there with an interest in the subject, but most are enticed by the lure of easy money.

That's what has me worried. Scams play on greed. If you want to run a successful scam, don't go after the guy who wants to work hard for his money. Scam the guy who wants to get rich quick – he's an easier target. Sell him the pyramid scheme, the mining company, the new technology – he's the sucker who'll buy it. Is that what's going on here?

'Are these the kind of people who change the world?' I'm asking myself. If I take a step back, the hard answer has to be no. But there is so much going on and so quickly, not just here but in the whole world of Bitcoin, that perhaps it's just a matter of waiting for the talented and competent to rise to the top.

There's another thing that has me concerned. I once took two of my kids to a happy-clappy church one Sunday (I wanted to get them singing more). Everyone was very, very friendly – worryingly so. They really wanted to convert you to their religion. Why, I'm not sure. So that you can be as happy as them, so that you go on the same emotional and psychological journey as them, so that their decisions are justified, and there are more people converted to the cause? All of those reasons and more, probably. But this auction reminds me of that church service.

I get talking to the chubby auctioneer. Adam is his name. Extremely polite and respectful – but cagey when I ask him what he does. He's a former fund manager from the City, I discover, and he's obviously been given stick for working there. I put him at ease by saying I write for *MoneyWeek* magazine.

It's impossible to make any money now as an independent, he says. He used to buy distressed companies, but there are no distressed companies any more. Low interest rates have meant that what should have died lives on. If he wants to set up a fund, the regulation is so onerous that he would need to raise £100 million to make it viable. That's impossible. Regulation has just re-enforced the monopolies of the banks. Big corporations like regulation because only they can afford it. It's a great big barrier to entry.

'But Bitcoin. There's none of that in Bitcoin. It's the future,' he says.

He's been called over to start another auction. A canny East End Jewish lad in his mid-30s, Paul, seems to be running things. I want to talk to him.

As the auction begins, Paul offers to buy 100 pounds' worth of bitcoin at £500 a coin. Wanting an excuse to talk him, I accept.

'One hundred pounds worth of bitcoin at 500. Sold,' calls out Adam.

Paul walks over to me.

'I've got to go to the cash point,' he says. 'Come on. I'll buy you a coffee. It's freezing. I need to warm up.'

The auction continues as we make our way to the cafe.

'Five hundred anyone?' shouts Adam the auctioneer from the table on which he's standing.

'Yes!' calls out one of the homeless/festival perennials, just as we pass them.

His mates snigger.

'Yes what?' says Adam.

'Er.'

The guy doesn't know. He looks at his mates. They snigger some more.

He is skinny, about 5'8", mid-twenties maybe, unshaven, wearing dirty grey tracksuit bottoms and not one, but two hoodies, both up over his head. Under the hoods, I make out a mischievous pair of dark eyes. A badge has been sown on to the outer hoody. It's a CND logo with the words 'Sean's Outpost Homeless Outreach'.[52]

'So he is homeless,' I think. I was right. How come the homeless are interested in Bitcoin?

Underneath 'Sean's Outpost Homeless Outreach' are the words 'Satoshi Forest', but I barely notice. I'm too busy wondering why on earth there are so many homeless at a Bitcoin meet.

The auction continues.

'Five twenty anyone?'

'Yes. Five twenty!' calls out the homeless dude.

'Bid or offer?' asks Adam.

'Er...Offer,' he guesses.

He's confused again. There's a pause as he tries to register the question. He looks to his mates for help.

'Do you want to buy or sell?' asks Adam, patiently.

He's stumped again. His mates snigger some more.

'Yes,' he guesses. Then he shouts out, 'Don't know.'

'You're not really cut out for capital markets, are you,' heckles my Jewish bitcoin-buyer Paul.

Everybody laughs.

But my first thought is concern. 'You can't take the piss out of a homeless person like that,' I think.

I go for my coffee with Paul. He's a derivatives trader – friendly, open, very knowledgeable, a fantastic source of information and contacts, and extremely confident. We swap email addresses, he sends me all sorts of links to interesting Bitcoin reading – and, by agreement, we never get round to the actual bitcoin exchange. Neither of us was that bothered.

'It was funny what you said to that homeless dude. How come there are so many homeless at a Bitcoin meet?' I ask.

'Homeless? Ha! That's Amir,' says Paul.

'Amir? Amir Taaki?'

Amir Taaki is one of the world's most dangerous/talented computer hackers – and one of Bitcoin's early coders. I thought he was in Spain. I have to talk to him.

We go back to the meet. Everybody else wants to talk to Amir as well. They are all asking him who Satoshi is.

Paul introduces me to one of Amir's mates. He can't be more than about 25, with the worst teeth I've ever seen. He doesn't talk much, just grunts in the manner of someone who's smoked too much weed.

'He's got more than 900 bitcoins,' Paul says.

'That's almost a million bucks!' I exclaim.

The grungy festivalgoer laughs gormlessly.

Another, from South Wales and the sweetest man you have ever met, explains how he runs Wales' only bitcoin-only store. He gives me a Bitcoin hat.

Finally, Paul introduces me to Amir.

We get talking. He is happy to meet for an interview. He tries to tap his email into my phone but makes a mess of it. If this guy's a computer genius, how can he not even tap an email into a phone?

Then he adds that he doesn't always reply to emails because he gets a lot. I know I need to pin him down there and then. I try to get his number. He's cagey.

'Can you do tomorrow tea-time?'

'Yes.'

Shit, I can't do tomorrow tea-time.

'How about in the morning at 11?'

'Yeah, OK. I'll get my girlfriend to wake me up.'

She approaches. Spanish. And, like all of them, grungy and friendly.

'This is Dominic. He's a writer. He's coming to do an interview in the morning. What's our address again?'

She tells me.

At 11 the following morning, I find myself standing outside a squat in Bow.

## Where Occupy and Bitcoin live together

It's an old industrial building with a big sign that says, 'Eastway Business Centre'. On a Sunday morning, the street is so deserted you feel like you're one of the few survivors in a zombie movie in which the population has been wiped out.

A tattered legal notice is taped aggressively t
windows. 'Section 144 LASPO does not apply' it :
to prevent the squatters being evicted).

I look around the building trying to find a bell
a front door. Everything is boarded up. I can see a ⌐ ple
of pairs of suspicious eyes looking at me from upstairs. I try
phoning Amir, but there is no answer.

After a good quarter of an hour, through a gap in some
boards, I finally spot Amir. He's brushing his teeth.

'I'm here to see Amir,' I say and am waved in.

At a guess, I'd say there are about 25 people living in the
squat. They're the same kind of 'festival goers' that were at
the meet the day before. A faint aroma of ganja wafts out of
a communal eating area. As I pass, I get a strange look from
a girl with dreadlocks, who seems surprised and a little ner-
vous to see me in there. Perhaps she feels I've come to throw
her out. Even in jeans I feel horribly overdressed.

Amir takes me upstairs to the living room. A couple is
asleep on a mattress on the floor in the corner.

'Won't they mind us talking?' I ask.

Amir says quite firmly, 'If we're disturbing them, they can
go somewhere else.'

As if in reply, they pull their sleeping bags over their
heads.

Amir asks another guy – unshaven, matted hair, grungy,
friendly – to bring us a chai. Amir seems to have a bit of
status in this place.

The chai arrives and the guy sits down with us. He wants
to listen to the interview. 'I'm interested in all this stuff,' he
says. It turns out he's one of the ringleaders in the Occupy
movement.

Amir starts talking.

I've always loved the way many inventions and discoveries happened by accident. Alexander Fleming didn't clean up one day and now we have penicillin. George Crum, a chef, got so infuriated by a customer who kept sending back his potatoes that he sliced them as thin and fried them as long as he dared – and we have the potato chip (or crisp). Wilhelm Roentgen was playing around with a light and some cathode ray tubes – and we have the X-ray.

Similarly, there's something of the accidental to Amir's involvement with Bitcoin.

The 26-year-old Anglo-Iranian, an experienced hacker, was earning his living playing online poker. But he was frustrated with poker sites. Their fees were too high, their software dated and insecure and their encryption systems so easy to break. 'It's a problem you give in school to like 12-year-olds,' he says. In other words, hackers could easily see other players' cards. Do you know anyone who's lost money playing online poker? Now you know why.

What's more, onerous regulations make it difficult for new entrants to start up poker sites, leading to what he calls a 'corrupt cartel' that controls the sector.

So he began to develop an open-source poker app, with a way of shuffling cards in a distributed way – meaning that only those playing the game need be involved in the shuffling. There was no longer any need to put trust in a house or central server.

But he needed a money system for the bets.

'I was searching around and talking,' he tells me. 'A mathematician gave me a bunch of different links. And one of them was this Bitcoin thing, and the site looked so sketchy. It was like a crappy blue webpage from, what, the nineties or something. And I was like, nah, it's a joke project – there are tons of those projects, where a coder makes them one weekend and then gets bored or forgets about it and there's nothing there.'

But Amir couldn't find anything better. With no other options and 'out of desperation', he came back to Bitcoin and took a second look. He looked at the software, chatted to the small community of developers working on the project – Sirius, Nefario, Keeper, and Gavin Andresen.

'Things started to make sense – this is real, this is fantastic,' he says, excitedly. 'I had loads of ideas for stuff that I always wanted to do, that was impossible, you know, new ways to do things, to fund open-source software, to create new projects. I was like wow, incredible. And for the next few days, I was telling everybody non-stop about it.'

He began working on various Bitcoin projects, but before long started to see problems in the Bitcoin software.

'If you have an open-source project,' he says, 'the way that you get everyone, the community, to participate, is to split things into small units, specialties and so on – simple bricks that fit together nicely. Each module, each component is simple to understand, you don't need to know what goes around it. You focus on making your brick as well as possible. And then all these bricks fit together to build a big complex system. But the Bitcoin software as it is, is just a big modular splotch, and if you change one thing, it affects all different things around it. Very complicated to deal with...I took the software and I started to improve it...we did a bunch of different things, but in the end I thought to myself, if Bitcoin s going to be such a big system, you know, on the world's infrastructure, we need a proper base to it. So I decided to rewrite the software – not something that I recommend. I would prefer to re-factor, but I chose to re-write the code.'

He looked at synchronicity, scalability, and privacy. All too aware that software degrades with time, he worked on the architecture so that it would 'maintain its integrity for as long as possible'.

## Rags to riches, comedy and charity

There are many such accidental stories in the evolution of Bitcoin. Not only has its evolution been chaotic, unplanned and organic, so is the community that has developed around it. It is an eclectic mix of all sorts from the computer whizz to the con artist to the economist; from the opportunist to the altruist to the activist. You can look around and see whatever you want to see – whether it's world-changers or no-hopers.

One student from Norway bought $27 worth in 2010 while studying for his degree. He forgot about them, and then remembered them three years later. That $27 had turned into $670,000. He sold half through MtGox and half through Bitcoin-24. He managed to get the money out of MtGox and bought a flat in Oslo. But the German authorities seized Bitcoin-24. With it went half of his fortune. 'I'm not so worried about that,' he says.

Another coder from Wales mined 7,500 bitcoins and then threw away his laptop. He spent many hours trawling the local rubbish dump trying to recover his fortune – without success.

Martti Malmi bought a beer from his friend for 10,000

BTC. His mate would later use those coins to buy a prime residence in central Helsinki.

Lily Allen was offered 100,000 bitcoins to perform on 3D chat website Second Life. She turned it down. That became, at one stage, a 100 million dollar fortune on which she missed out.

Charlie Shrem, who once hacked into the University of Ghana website and then wrote a white paper on their security flaws, was an early Bitcoin adopter. He made himself enough money to buy a pukka New York pad, and an even more pukka bar, will only employ people if they drink or smoke weed with him, founded a $40 million company and now finds himself under house arrest on money-laundering charges related to the Silk Road. He's still only 24.

Shrem has never even met his business partner, Gareth Nelson. Nelson is an Asperger's sufferer from Wrexham, who's now worth millions.

Olivier Janssens now flies from London to his new home in Monaco by private jet – paid for in bitcoins.

On my hunt for amusing Bitcoin stories, one chap emailed me, saying: 'I bought $8,000 worth of Litecoin at $2.30 back in June, and when Bitcoin skyrocketed to $1,240, Litecoin went to $52.00. I made $140,000, cashed out $70,000 and bought a new Range Rover. I now drive a Range Rover because of what people laugh at and call fake money.'

But with the failure of companies such as MtGox, you can bet there are many stories that are as disheartening as the above are amusing.

The world of crypto-currencies (there are now over 300 altcoins) has attracted all sorts of crooks and fraudsters, as well as those who religiously think they are changing the world. There are scams and get-rich-quick schemes galore. It has become a free-for-all, like the gold rushes of the Wild West. Over time, things should settle.

But one of the things you quickly notice is the sense of humour to it all. Many altcoins are based around a joke – 'Coinye West', for example. (When my father read this he asked, 'What's the joke?')

Many are simply in it for the laugh.

Dogecoin is, according to its website, 'an open source peer-to-peer cryptocurrency, favored by Shiba Inus worldwide'. (Shibu Inus are petite Japanese dogs that have a surprised look on their faces.) The currency is, apparently, based on an internet meme about a dog's inner thoughts. This has led to a heated discussion about the pronunciation of the word 'doge'. Is the G hard as in 'doggy'? Or is it soft as in 'refuge'. 'It's only a matter of time', says journalist Victoria McNally, 'before this discussion becomes all-out war in the style of GIF vs JIF.'[53]

In a reference to the much-loved 1993 comedy *Cool Runnings*, the Dogecoin community raised the funds to send the Jamaican bobsled team to the 2014 Winter Olympics. They then did the same for an Indian luge contender Shiva Keshavan. He would become the 2014 Winter Olympics 'underdoge'.

The community raised money earlier in the year for a water charity in Kenya. One person was able to donate $14,000 worth of coins with one tweet. The implications of that kind of ease of payment are enormous. Underlying Dogecoin, as well as technological advances, is a generosity of spirit.

Long may the spirit continue.

# 5

# HOW A COMPUTER NERD BECAME THE FBI'S MOST WANTED DRUG DEALER

*'You'd make a wonderful Dread Pirate Roberts.'*
— William Goldman, The Princess Bride

Imagine a website, like Amazon or eBay, but for drugs.

Not just drugs, but anything you can think of that's illegal: forged passports, counterfeit money, weapons even.

You type in what you're looking for, and up come the names of various sellers. You choose one you like, place your order, pay your money and a day or two later whatever you ordered shows up in a brown envelope.

There are at least 25 sites like this now in operation. The first was the Silk Road. A New York senator called it 'the most brazen attempt to peddle drugs online that we have ever seen'.[54]

Bitcoin made it possible.

I should say that, like our glorious Prime Minister, I may have erred while at university. But now, aged 44, my desire for most of the goods offered on Silk Road has faded. But that didn't stop my curiosity, and back in 2013 when I first heard about the site, I went online to take a look.

You found the website using an encrypted browser on the anonymous Tor network – in order to keep your whereabouts and identity hidden. You registered just as you would register at Amazon or eBay (but best not with your real name). You typed in what you were looking for and up came your desired item offered by different merchants in varying quantities. You could buy forged passports, driving licences, student ID, erotica, books, academic papers, apparel, electronic items, art, jewellery, lifetime memberships to Spotify – just about anything you can think of, most of it dodgy. At one brief stage, I believe weapons were also sold, but this was discontinued in 2012. It's not clear why. Some say it was lack of profitability, others say it was a reaction to shootings in the US, others put it down to simple fear.

The essence of the site was narcotics. Ninety-five per cent of the stuff on the site I had never even heard of. I bet you haven't either. 25i-NBome Blotters (HPBCD Complexed)? Psilocbe cyanescens? Haizenberg's Lord Shivas? Salvador Dalis? Superman Pills? Red Jokers? Dbol Dianabol Methandrostenolone? Goodness knows what most of this stuff was and what it could do to you.

Like eBay or Amazon, buyers and sellers, as well as the items they were supplying, had feedback ratings next to their account names, based on past trades. For example, Trader X might have got a five-star rating with a comment such as, 'Great stuff. Arrived quickly, as described. Thank you. A+' – or 'Rubbish gear, bad seller, one star'. You could tell if someone was a good or bad trader, and you could vet them.

Whatever you may think about drug laws, the site worked. People were able to trade peacefully in a way that, for the most part, satisfied both buyer and seller. The feedback system was conducive to good conduct. I liked the fact that a site like the Silk Road was able to exist outside the law and to self-regulate peacefully without the intervention of the benevolent hand of the state.

To test things out, I bought a small amount of cannabis (don't tell the authorities) from a vendor by the name of Mr Clonk. Lo and behold, two or three days later, said tiny amount arrived in a nondescript brown envelope. I would far rather do this (and even have my children do this) than have to go to some dark alleyway in some shady part of town at night.

The speed of growth of the site was testament to people's needs for the service it provided. From its inception in 2011 to its demise in autumn 2013, some $1.2 billion's worth of transactions are said to have taken place (this statistic depends on what bitcoin price you use, of course. You could use $10 or $1,200). Carnegie Mellon University professor Nicolas Christin ran a comprehensive analysis of the site in August 2012 and estimated sales of $15 million per year. In July 2013, he said, 'Somewhere between $30 million and $45 million a year would not surprise me. It may even be more.'[55] There were some 957,000 registered user accounts. I bet even the likes of Google, Amazon, eBay, Twitter, or Facebook would have struggled to compete with those kinds of numbers in their first two years of trading.

The site was run by the Dread Pirate Roberts. If you've seen *The Princess Bride*, you'll know that the Dread Pirate Roberts is William Goldman's notorious pirate, who 'takes no prisoners' and is 'feared across the seven seas' for his ruthlessness and swordsmanship. The Dread Pirate Roberts, it turns out, is not one man, but a succession of them. A Dread Pirate Roberts, when he is ready to retire, would pass the name and reputation to a chosen successor.

In other words, the person behind the Silk Road, the Dread Pirate Roberts, could – in theory – be anyone. And it appears there have been several already.

But it also looks like the most famous of them is now behind bars.

## The millionaire drugs kingpin with a soft spot for Austrian economics

In October 2013, after over a year of cyber-detective work, five plain-clothes FBI agents walked into the Glen Park Library in San Francisco. They made their way to the science fiction section. There a skinny 29-year-old man with jeans and a T-shirt was sitting at his laptop chatting with someone online (unknown to him, it was an FBI stooge). The library staff heard a crash. Poking their heads round the shelves, they saw him being pressed up against the window and handcuffed. He was, the FBI said, the Dread Pirate Roberts, reported to own over $30 million worth of bitcoins, to earn about $20,000 a day and to have amassed an $80 million fortune in 13 months. But he was in the Glen Park Library for the free wifi.

The man they arrested was Ross Ulbricht, a 29-year-old from Austin, Texas. He is hardly the millionaire kingpin of the Hollywood variety. Rather, he's a handsome nerd, a former physics student, living in a sub-let San Francisco room for $1,200 a month, for whom, according to an old college buddy, 'bathing is optional'.[56]

'He's a hippie. That's the best way I can describe him,' said his friend Jaspreet Sidhu. 'Ross was the guy who had stinky feet, that wore shorts – a shirt if you were lucky. He's one of the kindest and most good-natured people I know. He loves animals. He loves nature. Good people make bad choices.'[57]

One of the first things you notice about Ulbricht online is his admiration for the economist Ludwig Von Mises and the Austrian School of economic theory – its free-market doctrines and its attitudes towards liberty.

On his YouTube channel, as well as links to bands he likes, there are links to Ron Paul speeches and videos from the Von Mises Institute.

In 2010 Ulbricht posted an essay on Facebook, *Thoughts on Freedom*. The final words read, 'Let us...build a world where we, and the generations that follow us, will be freer than any that have come before!'[58]

On his LinkedIn profile he says, since completing his studies in 2010, he wants 'to use economic theory as a means to abolish the use of coercion and agression amongst mankind...The most widespread and systemic use of force is amongst institutions and governments, so this is my current point of effort. The best way to change a government is to change the minds of the governed...To that end I am creating an economic simulation to give people a first-hand experience of what it would be like to live in a world without the systemic use of force.'[59]

His 'simulation' was, say the FBI, the black market website, the Silk Road.

Indeed, the first thing you read when you came to the

Silk Road was the welcome from the Dread Pirate Roberts, in which he declared that economist Ludwig von Mises had provided 'the philosophical underpinnings' for the site. Roberts' signature even included a link to the Von Mises Institute website.

The Dread Pirate Roberts, at one stage, even started up a book club, saying:

> We will focus on agorism, counter-economics, anarcho-capitalism, Austrian economics, political philosophy, freedom issues and related topics. My hope is that through this, we will discover what we stand for and foster a culture of peace, prosperity, justice and freedom. There is so much double-speak and misinformation in the world today that we must take our education into our own hands, and defend our minds with reason and critical thinking.[60]

The Dread Pirate Roberts and Ulbricht seem to have had rather a lot in common.

Having split up with his girlfriend in November 2011, Ulbricht moved to Australia to stay with his older sister for several months. If he was the Dread Pirate Roberts, he was running the site from there. His sister thought he was trading currencies for a living (and he may well have been to provide the hedging functionality of the site). Then he came to San Francisco.

He went on one date with a woman he met on OKCupid and passed out drunk at the end of it. He paid his rent in cash, told his flat mates he was Australian and that his name was Josh, and pretty much cut himself off from friends and family back home. But he seemed to like San Francisco. 'Paradise is here or nowhere' he posted on Facebook.

The internet is a dangerous place. Often you do not know who you are talking to, and you cannot vet them as you would if you were to see them in person. You can become victim to all sorts of persuasion, influence and doctrine that psychologists are only just starting to study, let alone understand. We are all vulnerable, but the young, impressionable and idealistic, cut off from their friends and family and detached from reality, are particularly so.

Now he was charged with drugs trafficking, money laundering and attempted murder.

A poster who went by the name of Altoid was the first person to mention the Silk Road on the internet. On January 27th 2011 he wrote on a magic mushroom forum – Shroomery.org:

> I came across this website called Silk Road. It's a Tor hidden service that claims to allow you to buy and sell anything online anonymously. I'm thinking of buying off it, but wanted to see if anyone here had heard of it and could recommend it.
>
> I found it through silkroad420.wordpress.com, which, if you have a tor browser, directs you to the real site at LINK REMOVED
>
> Let me know what you think...[61]

Two days later, Altoid found a thread at BitcoinTalk, discussing the logistics of trading drugs using Bitcoin. The thread had been dead for over a month, but he revived it:

> What an awesome thread! You guys have a ton of great ideas. Has anyone seen Silk Road yet? It's kind of like an anonymous amazon.com. I don't think they have heroin on there, but they are selling other stuff. They basically use bitcoin and tor to broker anonymous transactions. It's at LINK REMOVED Those not familiar with Tor can go to silkroad420 .wordpress.com for instructions on how to access the .onion site.
>
> Let me know what you guys think

Altoid later deleted the post, but it had been quoted in the replies, which meant it would remain.

Altoid continued posting at BitcoinTalk for several months. He was trading bitcoins with mixed success – it appeared he had sold too soon on some occasions, but he also claimed to have made $200,000 on one trade.[62] He also had issues getting money out of MtGox.

From June to October, he would go quiet. Then, on October 11th 2011, he would write a post that everyone would ignore, except one person – an FBI Special Agent named Christopher Tarbell. That post would be the beginning of the end for Ulbricht.

> Hello, sorry if there is another thread for this kind of post, but I couldn't find one. I'm looking for the best and brightest IT pro in the bitcoin community to be the lead developer in a venture backed bitcoin startup company. The ideal candidate would have at least sev-

eral years of web application development experience, having built applications from the ground up. A solid understanding of oop and software architecture is a must. Experience in a start-up environment is a plus, or just being super hard working, self-motivated, and creative.

Compensation can be in the form of equity or a salary, or somewhere in-between.

If interested, please send your answers to the following questions to rossulbricht at Gmail dot com

1) What are your qualifications for this position?

2) What interests you about bitcoin?

From there, we can talk about things like compensation and references and I can answer your questions as well. Thanks in advance to any interested parties. If anyone knows another good place to recruit, I am all ears.[63]

The same Altoid who had made the first mention of the Silk Road on the internet had left his name and email address – rossulbricht@gmail.com. And the FBI would read it all.

He then left another clue.

In 2012, Ulbricht opened an account in his own name at a question-and-answer website for programmers called Stack Overflow. He posted 12 lines of computer code and asked for advice about a problem. He then changed his username to Frosty and the registered email address to frosty@frosty.com.

But a revised version of that same code was used on the Silk Road website, along with encryption keys that end with 'frosty@frosty'.

The FBI had their prime suspect. Now to snare him.

## How a nerd was tricked into becoming a murderer

An FBI agent, posing as a drug dealer, emailed the Dread Pirate Roberts directly, seeking help finding a buyer for a kilogram of cocaine. Roberts is said to have found a buyer – one of his employees, Curtis Clark Green. Green sent $27,000 of bitcoins and arranged shipment, amazingly, to his home.

When the coke showed up, so did the FBI and Green was arrested.

Roberts must have trusted the supposed drug dealer (the FBI agent) with whom he was communicating. It's not yet clear how much he was goaded and how much he knew about Green's arrest, but he wrote to the FBI agent, 'I'd like him beat up, then forced to send the bitcoins he stole back'.[64] The agent offered to do it.

The following day Roberts wrote, says the FBI, 'now that he's been arrested, I'm afraid he'll give up info...Can you change the order to execute rather than torture?' Roberts said he had 'never killed a man or had one killed before, but it is the right move in this case'.[65] An $80,000 fee for the hit was agreed.

$40,000 was sent from Technocash Limited in Australia (where Ulbricht was with his sister) to a bank account at Capital One in Washington. The Dread Pirate Roberts was emailed staged photographs of the killing. 'A little disturbed, but I'm OK', he wrote. 'I'm new to this...I don't think I've done the wrong thing'. Another $40,000 was deposited. And the grounds for the attempted murder charge were laid.

Then there would be another bizarre and rather frightening twist in the tale. Roberts soon requested a second killing.

A Silk Road user called FriendlyChemist made a blackmail threat. He demanded the Dread Pirate Roberts pay him $500,000 or he would release all sorts of personal data he hacked from the Silk Road's online community.

Another Silk Road user, Redandwhite (an alias for Hell's Angels), then emailed claiming that they were owed money by FriendlyChemist. Roberts, it is claimed by the FBI, invited Redandwhite to start dealing through the Silk Road, 'If you don't already sell here on Silk Road, I'd like you to consider becoming a vendor'.[66]

When FriendlyChemist began demanding funds again, Roberts wrote to Redandwhite, 'I wouldn't mind if he was executed...I have the following info and am waiting on getting his address. I would like to put a bounty on his head, if it's not too much trouble for you'.[67]

Redandwhite quoted a price of between $150,000 and $300,000 to kill the blackmailer. Roberts said, 'Don't want to be a pain here, but the price seems high...Not long ago, I had a clean hit done for $80K. Are the prices you quoted the best you can do?'

They settled on 1,670 bitcoins – about $150,000 – and according to the block chain that money was sent. Roberts then handed over the real name of FriendlyChemist and his address where he lived with his wife and three kids.

Redandwhite did the job, sent in a photo of the done deed

with, lying next to the body, a piece of paper with some numbers on it that Ulbricht had asked for. Redandwhite would go on to kill another four people who were involved in this conspiracy, according to emails, for a fee of half a million.[68]

There is no record of any related murders having taken place in British Colombia or elsewhere at that time. Investigators say there is no evidence anyone died, despite almost three quarters of a million dollars alleged to have been spent.

But when Ulbricht was arrested, he found himself wanted for six charges of attempted murder.

The FBI found that the IP address used to access the Silk Road was an internet cafe 500 feet from where Ulbricht lived. How they managed to do this given the encryption involved is not known. Some believed the weakness lay in Ulbricht's code. Others feel they may have been tipped off.

Google records showed Ulbricht would regularly access his Gmail account from this same IP address and both the Silk Road and Ulbricht's Gmail account were accessed several times on the same day in June. 'This evidence places the administrator of Silk Road, that is, DPR [Dread Pirate Roberts], in the same approximate geographic location, on the same day, as Ulbricht'.[69]

There was another twist. Shortly before, customs officials opened a package from Canada containing fake IDs, all with Ulbricht's face on them. The FBI knew that the Dread Pirate Roberts had been asking questions about fake ID. Customs visited the address and found Ulbricht. Ulbricht told them anyone could hypothetically go to a website called the Silk Road and buy fake ID there. What a thing to say.

He would soon be arrested.

I'm writing this in March 2014. The attempted murder

charges relating to Redandwhite have been dropped, presumably because it is obvious Ulbricht was being scammed. But the Curtis Green charges are still live, as are charges of large-scale criminal enterprise, drug trafficking, hacking and money laundering.

Ulbricht has pleaded not guilty. A campaign has begun to help him raise the money to fight his case, Free Ross Ulbricht – freeross.org.

## Why Bitcoin will end the war on drugs

The FBI congratulated themselves. Over a year's work and they had got their man. It was a great victory. The bitcoin price fell from $140 to $110 in just a few hours. The Silk Road had been busted. FBI agent Christopher Tarbell was hailed as the 'Elliott Ness of cyberspace'.[70]

Many libertarians saw it as a loss. They need not have been despondent. Within two weeks, three copycat sites had opened up, including Silk Road 2.0 – run by – you guessed it – the Dread Pirate Roberts.

When I first wrote this chapter I could find 17 different so-called 'dark sites', where you can buy drugs with bitcoins on the Tor network: Silk Road 2.0, Black Market Reloaded, Pandora Market, Agora Market, TorMarket, The Marketplace (the M of 'Market' is the McDonald's M), the Three Hares Bazaar, the RoadSilk, White Rabbit Marketplace, Outlaw Market, Bungee Discreet Global Mailorder, Blue Sky, Modern Culture, Budster, Dutchy and Utopia. At Utopia I noticed you could also buy a guide to hacking ATMs, $100 of counterfeit dollars for $35 together with instructions on how to spend them, and 'untraceable, 3D-printed guns'.

At the point of final edit, there now seem to be 25 different sites. Meanwhile, of the above, Black Market Reloaded has shut down, TorMarket disappeared in a scam, as did Budster, Three Hares doesn't seem to have ever actually operated, RoadSilk has renamed itself Pirate Market, White Rabbit I'm advised is currently a scam, and Utopia has been busted by Dutch police.

These are just the ones a cursory search has revealed to me. If it took the FBI over a year to track down and arrest Ulbricht – assuming he is the Dread Pirate Roberts – how long and how much manpower will it take them to track down and arrest the people behind these 25 sites (who, one assumes, won't make the same mistakes the Dread Pirate Roberts did)?

There are now even directories of online Tor market-places – for example, All Markets Vendor Directory, run by one 'El Presidente', and DarkList.

DarkList said it was aiming to be as 'uninteresting' to law enforcement as possible. 'We don't sell product', says an administrator. 'The brief history of dark web marketplaces shows that there are three possible outcomes: incarceration, scam, or get hacked – none of which are congruent with our aspirations or morals'.[71]

He's right. The Silk Road was shut down and Ross Ulbricht was incarcerated. Sites like Atlantis, Project Black Flag and Sheep Marketplace all saw their administrators make off with their clients' money. Silk Road 2.0 was hacked to the tune of $2.7 million worth of bitcoins.

If a dark market should close down (as, sooner or later, seems inevitable), DarkList says it will help the site's cus-tomers reconnect with their dealers. There are even functions to message them and send them bitcoins. 'So, instead of being the Wal-Mart of drugs, we are more interested in a model analogous to Yelp. I can tell you that we have limited our functionality, as well as monetization opportunities, to mitigate the interest of those wishing to enforce their laws'.[72]

'Let's face it – buying and selling anonymously on the Dark Web is currently in a volatile state' reads the tag on the homepage. 'We built this directory so that you can always have a way to stay in contact with those you love'.

Darklist operates on Tor to hide users' identities. Rather than replace the markets, Darklist links to them, taking a 2.5% commission. Its operations are not such a clear-cut violation of the law – they are selling information, not drugs. It makes enforcement of law that much more difficult and complicated. As laws change to try to keep up, coders find new ways round them. Technology is moving faster than the law.

And guess what? Since writing this, Darklist has already gone offline. Now all the rage is about the Grams directory and search-engine.

If the Silk Road or any of these other sites used government money – pounds, euros or dollars – to effect transactions, they would be considerably harder to operate – and considerably easier to police.

Bitcoin is not completely anonymous, as many mistakenly think it is – if I know you and I know your wallet address, I can track your spending – but there is the potential to be much more anonymous than traditional banking, if so desired. Completely anonymous dark wallets are currently being developed – by Amir Taaki among others – as well as various dark coins. But Bitcoin is considerably less restricted than fiat money systems.

The ease with which money can be sent, and the potential to hide identity, has changed black markets – and led to a proliferation of them. It will take huge resources to police them all. In all probability, Bitcoin will lead to changes in law – changes that already seem to be slowly happening.

People are always going to want to buy drugs. Bitcoin is enabling them. Unless the authorities launch a War on Bitcoin – which due to its decentralized nature will be a very hard war to win – it seems they will lose the War on Drugs once and for all. Bitcoin may be what ends it.

# 6

# WHO IS SATOSHI NAKAMOTO?

*Satoshi is everywhere and nowhere.*

*Satoshi could be all of us, or none of us.*

*Satoshi came from nowhere and disappeared to nowhere, but his coins are everywhere.*

*Satoshi has no past, no future, and no present, but his creation is immortal.*

*Satoshi is an idea. Satoshi has inspired all of us. Satoshi is legend.*

— em3rgentOrdr

The *Mary Rose*, Big Foot, the Bermuda Triangle, the Loch Ness Monster, the Babushka Lady. These are just a few of the great mysteries that have bewitched, bothered and bewildered.

To that list you can add 'Who is Satoshi Nakamoto?'

He has invented an entirely new digital system of money with the potential to change the world as we know it. He has watched it grow to a market cap of at one stage over 12 billion dollars – equivalent to the currency value of a small country. He has half the internet nosing about and trying to figure out who he is. And he is worth over half a billion dollars.

Yet he has managed to stay completely unknown and anonymous. It is almost unbelievable.

Anyone can claim to be him. Anyone can deny it. If someone pins him down with arguments and evidence that 'demonstrate' his identity, he can go on denying it. Without access to his computer records, nothing can be proven.

I have spent a lot of time on this detective hunt – way more than I anticipated or intended. But the mystery is overpoweringly compelling. Who is this computer genius who never reveals himself? Why the secret? Does he have something else to hide?

And there are personal dilemmas I've had to grapple with. If I have found out who Satoshi Nakamoto is, should I say? He has taken great steps to hide his identity. Anonymity and privacy are obviously what he wants. Should I be the one to violate that?

Is Bitcoin undermined if we suddenly know who the creator is?

Or is it in the public interest to know, given how much is now invested in Bitcoin and the power he has (he owns about 5% of all coins) to move the price?

## How America's most famous news magazine got the wrong Satoshi

Founded in 1933, *Newsweek* came to rival *Time* as America's most famous news magazine. Perhaps the highlight of its impressive history was the breaking of the Monica Lewinsky scandal that so undermined Bill Clinton's presidency.

But the web changed the way we consume news. It challenged the behemoths that had controlled the media. *Newsweek*, like so many others, failed to embrace the new technology and it fell into drastic decline. Despite numerous attempts to re-format the magazine and change focus, by 2010 falling sales were such that it was sold for a dollar.

December 31st 2012 was the publication date of the last printed issue of the magazine.

But, in March 2014, another attempt was made to revamp it. The print edition would be re-launched, and the editors needed a big story for the front cover. They decided that big story would be the revelation of Satoshi Nakamoto's identity.

Reporter Leah McGrath Goodman was given the job. She spent two months on the story – and hired two forensic scientists to help her.

Combing a database that contained the registration cards of naturalized US citizens, she found a Satoshi Nakamoto. Born in Japan in 1949, he emigrated to the US ten years later. But after graduating from California State Polytechnic at 23, he dropped 'Satoshi', changing his name to 'Dorian Prentice Satoshi Nakamoto' and signing it 'Dorian S. Nakamoto'.

She delved deeper. Speaking to Nakamoto's family and work colleagues, she put together a profile. Here was a libertarian, a man who would always expound 'on politics and world affairs',[73] a maths genius who loved technology, built computers at home and told his children off if they came near them, a recluse who would work all hours from before his children woke up till after they went to sleep. His work experience included defensive electronics and communication for the US military, computer engineering for financial information services and software engineering for the Federal Aviation Administration in New Jersey in the wake of the terrorist attacks on September 11th. He ticked a lot of boxes.

But then he stopped replying to her emails. She went to his house. He refused to talk and called the police on her. Goodman was convinced she had her man hiding in plain sight and she broke her story. 'Standing before me, eyes downcast', she wrote, was 'the father of Bitcoin...tacitly acknowledging his role in the project'. *Newsweek* had a huge scoop, trumpeted the fact and the story went viral.

She even published his address and pictures of his house, a ramshackle affair in a poor Southern Californian suburb.

Satoshi's game was up.

The world's media descended on Nakamoto's home. Here they found a confused, gentle-looking, sickly and retired 64-year-old Japanese man who looked like a comically eccentric professor. He had not heard of Bitcoin, he said, until three weeks ago when Goodman first mentioned it to him. As journalists bombarded him with cameras and questions outside his home, he declared he would only talk to one person, who must buy him a free lunch. 'I want my free lunch,' he said.

Nakamoto left with an Associated Press journalist. Such was the frenzy, there was an actual car chase across Los Angeles.

I read the article despondently, thinking my many months of research into Satoshi and the 12,000 words I had written on the subject were wasted.

But something didn't ring right. Goodman's article had a slightly nasty tone to it, as if she was getting her own back on Nakamoto for the fact he had called the police on her. There was too much bias and too many projections of her imagination. 'He stands not with defiance,' she said, 'but with the slackness of a person who has waged battle for a long time and now faces a grave loss.' That's a subjective interpretation. He might just have had bad posture. Why insult him?

Her tone was too confident; arrogant, even – anyone who's spent fruitless months on the Satoshi trail is soon taught humility. His age didn't seem right, either. Sixty-four is too old (as I'll explain). And, most glaringly of all, there was no mention of Cypherpunks in her story, nor even any suggestion that she had investigated this crucial theme.

The web quickly got to work. Examples were found of things Dorian Nakamoto had written – Amazon reviews, letters to magazines, local authorities. His prose was a far cry from the meticulous accuracy of Satoshi's.

His Amazon reviews were actually published under his own name. Would the secretive Satoshi have done that? Dorian was, it seems, not satisfied with a razor he had bought, saying:

> after even 2 shaves, it begans to dull. i can only get about 12 – 15 shaves vs. no name K-mart lasting 35 shaves. and i wipe any moisture off the blades for both, the no-name brand and the merkur despite the latter reads no need.
>
> remember, the major cause of poor lasting edge is the rust u don't c.

the merkur blades r too expensive to boot! i won't buy it again. Warning: K-mart had other no-name blades that didn't last either but this last one bought about 4 months ago is still bood, blade after blade.[74]

He was rather more happy with some Royal Danish cookies:

royal danish butter cookies in a big 4lb round blue tin can

it has lots of buttery taste.

the shipment went well. i've had a nice comment from my kids. it's a perfect xmas and i would say, for other occasions.[75]

An email was found that he'd written to the Metro transit system:

hi!

i vote for underground railing for above project. the project should be done so the business shops's income from clients would be minimally affected.

good secruity system against usage of rail as a get away means from the low income generated theives/criminals from area of east LA et. al must be also put in place regardless of the rail passage chosen.

i like the idea of using an economical and modern rail to little tokyo from sierra madregold line station. the parking fee + gasoline costs $10 now to get there from my home and i would go there more often with my mother for shoppings.

dorian nakamoto

a recident from temple city, calif[76]

The above reviews and email are published as written, with errors uncorrected.

The idea that the person who wrote these reviews also produced the more than 80,000 words of unblemished prose that Satoshi produced is laughable. Forbes magazine called in a stylometrics expert, as if such a thing were needed, by the name of John Noecker Jr. He verified that the person who wrote the above was not the same person who composed the Bitcoin white paper and all Satoshi's other posts.

Coders, too, were sure this was not the man who had coded Bitcoin. The techno entrepreneur and writer Anil Dash summed up their view when he said on Twitter, 'I haven't found a single person who codes who thinks Dorian is credible as the creator'.

While Satoshi was busy coding Bitcoin, Dorian, it seems from the communication he had with a particular magazine,[77] was busy with *his* hobby – building model train sets.

At his free lunch with the AP journalist, apparently he referred to Bitcoin as 'Bitcom'.

Why did Goodman fail to see all this?

She did not look hard enough, is the answer. She could have delved further and discovered these writings of Dorian. She could have spoken to coders. She could have put her findings to the Bitcoin community and exploited the vast communal knowledge therein. They would soon have put her right. But she didn't. She wanted her big story and she had a deadline.

This is something I have encountered time after time on the trail of Satoshi. You find someone who fits the profile, and then find heaps of circumstantial evidence to confirm your bias, but you ignore the evidence that discredits it. It's the prosecutor's fallacy.

Within a few hours, Goodman's research had been debunked. The Nakamotos might have shared the same name, but the parallels ended there. *Newsweek* looked bad, Goodman's reputation lay in tatters and a shy, retiring man's life had been up-ended.

Goodman was castigated for publishing Nakamoto's address and using such circumstantial evidence. Gavin Andresen, who had given a lengthy interview for the article, said on Twitter: 'I'm disappointed Newsweek decided to dox (expose personal information) the Nakamoto family, and regret talking to Leah.'

The respected financial author Nassim Taleb was rather less reserved: 'Ms Goodman,' he said to her in a conversation on Twitter, 'there is something despicable about you and your profession. Voyeurism is not journalism...Your profession of violating people's privacy for profit? You call that journalism or voyeurism?'

Then something amazing happened. After over three years of silence, Satoshi himself re-appeared.

He posted on the P2P forums, one of the first public forums where he had mentioned Bitcoin five years previously, using the same email address he had used back then. He said, simply, 'I am not Dorian Nakamoto.'[78]

Now, of course, there was speculation as to whether this

was the real Satoshi acting out of the goodness of his heart to protect Dorian, Dorian himself posing as himself to protect himself or a hacker.

But Dorian, it seems, might still have been dealing with the media at the time of the posting. And P2P stated that Satoshi's account did not appear to have been hacked. (If it had, why just the one post?)

Was Satoshi watching?

Goodman is by no means the first person to try and track down Satoshi. Joshua Davis of the *New Yorker* spent four months on the job back in 2011. He was first led to a doctoral student from the University of Dublin called Michael Clear. Then he thought it might be a Finnish economic sociologist named Dr Vili Lehdonvirta.

Professor Adam Penenberg from New York University went on the job for business magazine *Fast Company* and concluded it was a trio of computer scientists – Neal J King, Charles Bry and Vladimir Oksman.

Andrew Smith spent several months on the job on behalf of the *Sunday Times*, describing it as the 'longest and most involving project' he'd ever worked on – 'not sure I've ever worked harder or longer on a piece...Bitcoin goes way deeper than we've realised'.[79] The tentative conclusion of his terrific piece was David Chaum, the inventor of Digicash.

All of the above names have failed stylometrics tests – in other words their prose does not match Satoshi's. None of them have a Cypherpunks background. It's not clear any of them have the right coding skills. And all of them, except Chaum, have publicly denied any connection. (See Appendix II for more on Chaum.)

Online there have been hundreds of blog posts and discussion groups and many thousands of man hours dedicated to pinning down this man. All have proved inconclusive.

Satoshi's identity is as bulletproof as his code.

I have ventured on this same journey that is doomed to failure. It has now taken me five months and counting. I've pored over the 80,000 words Satoshi wrote in the three years he was active online, looking for clues. What unusual words did he use? Does he make any spelling mistakes? Does he have any quirky grammatical habits? I've analysed it in such detail I can tell you where he places brackets, how he uses hyphens, even how many spaces he uses now and used to use after a full stop – all in the hope of finding idiosyncrasies that appear in the writing of other prominent Cypherpunks or academics.

This book is late because of it. Here's what I've found.

## My first instinct

Often it's good to go with your first instinct. For reasons I cannot begin to explain, even after you research something in depth, your first instinct is frequently proved correct.

At first, I thought Satoshi was Hal Finney, the veteran programmer – he of re-usable proof of works. My reasoning was simple.

When Satoshi first announced Bitcoin on the cryptography mailing list, nobody replied. The message was ignored for two days. In the short-attention-span land of the web, two days is a long time to wait for some feedback on something you've spent 18 months working on. Two days is a long time to wait when you might have nailed something Cypherpunks have been dreaming about for 20 years.

The first reply came from Finney. Was he replying to himself in order to generate some interest and discussion – to bump his thread? Replying to your own posts is not uncommon in this regard. It is known as 'sock-puppeting'. I've even done it myself.

Satoshi is almost certainly too clever – and too patient – for that. He has his emotions under control. But let us pursue this line of thinking a little further.

Finney was born in 1956 – in that same two-year golden window when the computer-scientist geniuses that would change the world were born – and spent his life working on cryptographic systems. He was number two to Phil Zimmerman, the pioneer in the field, for many years at the Pretty Good Privacy (PGP) Corporation, where they developed the most widely used email encryption software in the world.

Such were his beliefs in privacy, freedom and Cypherpunk, Finney was known to spend many nights writing and developing code for free, just because he believed in the work.

In 1993, he published the paper, 'Detecting Double-Spending'.[80] Solving the double-spending problem was of course the key problem with digital cash. It was what Satoshi was so excited about when he proposed Bitcoin. In 2004, Finney developed the 'reusable proof-of-work' (RPOW) system, which coders regarded as a brilliant step forward – but his system never saw any economic use until Bitcoin.

Finney is one of the few people to have the background and expertise to have developed Bitcoin – but he is also an obvious person to take an immediate interest.

In his very first reply to Satoshi's announcement, he wrote:

As an amusing thought experiment, imagine that Bitcoin is successful and becomes the dominant payment system in use throughout the world. Then the total value of the currency should be equal to the total value of all the wealth in the world. Current estimates of total worldwide household wealth that I have found range from $100 trillion to $300 trillion. With 20 million coins, that gives each coin a value of about $10 million.[81]

Of course, that is just an amusing thought experiment. It's like gold bugs explaining why gold is going to go to $70,000 an ounce because of US debt. But could it also be somebody trying to get others excited?

And, by the way, 'thought experiment' is an expression Satoshi himself uses[82] – though it is not uncommon in coding circles.

Indeed, the writing of Finney and Satoshi is similar – a similar calm understated tone, similar use of language, similar punctuation habits: two spaces after a full stop, for example (this kind of detective work gets very precise). John Noecker Jr., chief scientific officer at text analysis experts Juola & Associates, compared Finney's writing with that of Satoshi – along with various other names who have been put forward as possible Satoshis. Noecker tells me that in every single experiment they carried out, Finney – along with one other name who I'll come to – was always the top performer.

Then I noticed both Finney and Satoshi had '@gmx.com' email addresses. (GMX is a free email provider based in Germany. Many Germans use GMX, while Americans and

British tend to gravitate towards Gmail, Hotmail or Yahoo). Was this just coincidence – or was it a clue?

## Why did Satoshi disappear?

In December 2010, Satoshi made his final post and then disappeared from the internet.

Why?

Perhaps to protect his anonymity in the face of rising interest from the media and, more significantly, the authorities: to protect his own safety as the WikiLeaks panic began to erupt.

There is also the possibility that he disappeared because he was ill.

In 2009, Finney was diagnosed with Lou Gehrig's disease – amyotrophic lateral sclerosis – the same disease from which Stephen Hawking suffers. It is, for the most part, fatal and claims its victims within two to five years. 'My symptoms were mild at first,' he says, 'and I continued to work, but fatigue and voice problems forced me to retire in early 2011. Since then the disease has continued its inexorable progression.'[83]

In March 2013 he said, 'Today, I am essentially paralyzed. I am fed through a tube, and my breathing is assisted through another tube. I operate the computer using a commercial eye-tracker system. It also has a speech synthesizer, so this is my voice now. I spend all day in my power wheelchair. I worked up an interface using an arduino so that I can adjust my wheelchair's position using my eyes. It has been an adjustment, but my life is not too bad. I can still read, listen to music, and watch TV and movies. I recently discovered that

I can even write code. It's very slow, probably 50 times slower than I was before. But I still love programming and it gives me goals.'[84]

Could a terrible illness be the reason Satoshi withdrew?

Finney was one of the first to mine bitcoins. What did he do with them?

> I mined several blocks over the next days. But I turned it off because it made my computer run hot, and the fan noise bothered me. In retrospect, I wish I had kept it up longer, but on the other hand I was extraordinarily lucky to be there at the beginning. It's one of those glass half full half empty things.
>
> The next I heard of Bitcoin was late 2010, when I was surprised to find that it was not only still going, bitcoins actually had monetary value. I dusted off my old wallet, and was relieved to discover that my bitcoins were still there. As the price climbed up to real money, I transferred the coins into an offline wallet, where hopefully they'll be worth something to my heirs. Those discussions about inheriting your bitcoins are of more than academic interest. My bitcoins are stored in our safe deposit box, and my son and daughter are tech savvy. I think they're safe enough. I'm comfortable with my legacy.[85]

Finney, it seems, has since sold many of his bitcoins in order to pay for medical care, many at around $100.[86] Satoshi does not appear to have spent his.

## Finney - yet another red herring

Finney was a key player in the development of Bitcoin, no doubt. He was one of the first to ask real questions. He managed to understand from the start the inner working of the Bitcoin protocol. He explored the weaknesses in the Bitcoin code – one of them is even named 'the Finney Attack'.[87] He had many exchanges with Satoshi on the Bitcoin forums as they progressed the code and developed new versions. He asked question after question. But these very exchanges show there were two people talking. On January 10th 2009, for example, Finney publicly complained to Satoshi that Bitcoin had crashed when he tried to receive a transaction. If it was his own code, and he was transacting with himself, he would surely have quietly fixed it himself.

Moreover, coders all agree that Finney's coding style – and the style of the comments written in the code – is different to Satoshi's. Also, Finney preferred to code in the language C, whereas Bitcoin is coded in C++. This is something Finney himself confirms: 'I've done some changes to the Bitcoin code, and my style is completely different from Satoshi's. I program in C, which is compatible with C++, but I don't understand the tricks that Satoshi used.'[88]

Shortly before the publication of this book, the *Forbes* journalist Andy Greenberg published an interview with Hal Finney.[89] Finney was now too ill to even speak – he could only raise his eyebrows to say yes. His son showed Greenberg fifteen email exchanges between Satoshi and Finney from

January 2009. They mainly focused on bugs Finney had found in the code, to which Satoshi replied with fixes (and notes of thanks).

Greenberg was also shown Finney's bitcoin wallet – with the transfers between Satoshi and Finney made back in 2009.

As Greenberg notes, the wallet evidence and the Gmail timestamps in the emails would have been hard to forge.

Bitcoin could not have happened without the work of Finney.

But Hal Finney is not Satoshi Nakamoto.

*Note: On August 28th, 2014, Hal Finney's life support machine was switched off and he passed away. His body has been cryonically preserved. My deepest and sincerest condolences go out to his family. He was a great man. May his soul rest in peace.*

## Profiling a genius - some broad brushstrokes

'I've had the good fortune to know many brilliant people over the course of my life,' said Finney, 'so I recognize the signs.'[90]

Satoshi is indeed brilliant.

His brilliance lies in the fact that he has reached such high levels of expertise in so many different fields – so much so that many believe he can't possibly be one person. He is a polymath. It is not just the breadth and depth of his knowledge, but, more importantly, its specificity that makes him unique.

In order to first conceive a new system of electronic cash, one would have to have an extensive knowledge of monetary history. Money is a subject that has found more interest in the last few years with the emergence of Bitcoin, the bull market in gold, the financial crisis and the growth of libertarianism, but, even so, it does not have broad appeal. In 2007–8, books and academic papers on the subject were few and far between.

How many of those who cared actually had the ability to design a system like this? It is one thing declaring what needs to be done; it is another putting it into practice.

Satoshi must have had expertise in computer coding, mathematics, databases, accounting, peer-to-peer systems, digital ownership, law, smart contracts, cryptography and monetary history.

He had to have had experience in academia. The act of submitting a white paper, its presentation, the impeccable referencing – it all denotes academia, even government.

It's also easy to infer from the way Bitcoin was launched that Satoshi had experience in open-source tech start-ups.

The resilience of the code suggests he had computer hacking experience. Moreover, his ability to keep his identity hidden, despite the fact that half the internet is trying to figure out who he is, suggests significant practical experience in staying anonymous. It also means he has the trust of those who know him, if anyone does, to keep his secret.

Then there's the matter of his prose. It is consistent and of such a high standard it seems he must have had experience as a writer – perhaps he was a blogger, an academic or an author. He was also quite humble and dismissive of his ability in this regard. 'I'm better with code than with words',[91] he said.

It's clear from his posts that he had the awareness to see the shortcomings of his system, and the patience not to try to do too much too quickly. He had the foresight to perceive problems before they arose and the meticulousness to pre-pare for them. He appears to have remained calm and mea-sured in the face of difficulty, but also of his own success. He treated those two imposters just the same. Signs of arrogance are hard to find.

Then there's the way that Bitcoin was introduced to the world. Satoshi seems to have been very adept at PR.

PR, like economics, is not an exact science. Sometimes something gains traction, sometimes it doesn't – and there's no explaining why. Bitcoin has been a PR masterstroke. It is still a tiny part of the world of finance, yet the coverage it has received is disproportionate to its size. Bitcoin gets more publicity than gold, which is the oldest form of money there is. Satoshi cannot take all of the credit for this. But he has to take some of it. He understood when to make his ideas known, at what point to release his creation into the open-source world and he had the self-effacement to let go of it for others to develop. He promoted his idea with huge under-statement – but the scheduled deflation of bitcoins (in other words that their value will likely increase) means there would be no shortage of bitcoin-holders to do the promoting for him.

So we can add an understanding of psychology to his list of qualities. His knowledge of how people on the internet, in the open source world and in large institutions work allowed him to progress his creation.

Finally, he has a certain honesty. Despite Bitcoin's simi-larities to a pyramid or Ponzi scheme, he never pumped-and-dumped his creation. Tempting though it must have been, he seems to have kept most of the bitcoins he mined (more on this later).

There are not many people like this.

From mathematics to computer programming to economics and monetary history to politics to PR and psychology to cryptography to business acumen and vision to plain old written English – in all of these fields he excelled. To cap it all, he's probably good-looking too.

It's too early in history to be drawing this sort of comparison, I know, but there are many parallels between Satoshi and Isaac Newton. Newton was a brilliant scientist and mathematician, of course. But he was also Master of the Royal Mint. He redesigned England's monetary system, putting us onto the gold standard on which Britain's colossal progress during the next 200 years was built.

As I continued my hunt for Satoshi, I started asking myself questions not just about *who* he could be...but also about *why* he did what he did?

Why did he not want to reveal his real name?

There are all sorts of possibilities.

Perhaps he thought his name might compromise the project in some way. Perhaps he would have risked his career by being associated with Bitcoin.

No doubt he had seen the persecution, often by government authorities, that had befallen other digital currency innovators, some of whom ended up behind bars. Perhaps he felt anonymity would help him avoid that.

Perhaps he got a thrill from being anonymous – a shadowy figure behind a mystery that would capture the world's imagination.

Perhaps he did not want the attention that might follow if the project was a success – be it from the media, the authorities or even criminals.

And what would motivate someone with the desire to create an open-source, decentralized form of non-government money?

Of course, personal financial gain is one factor. But if that was the only reason, you would expect Satoshi to have sold a lot more of his bitcoins than he has.

Another possible reason might be the challenge: can I overcome this hitherto unsolved technological problem that has stumped so many?

Plain ambition might have been a factor. The motivation might also have been altruistic – to help those people that are shut out of the current financial system. Or it could have been political and ideological. He may have thought our system of money was broken – it benefited the few at the expense of the many, it was creating economic distortion – and he wanted to fix it.

There are only two worlds where that level of extreme monetary ideology can be found – amongst libertarians and Cypherpunks.

## How much of a Cypherpunk was Satoshi?

When the moment came to make his invention known to the world, Satoshi could have announced it anywhere. On a tech forum, on a dedicated website, in a newspaper, to academia.

But of all the forums in the world available to him, he chose the cryptography mailing list.

Why? And what does that tell us?

The original Cypherpunks mailing list had been disbanded several years earlier. Excess spam, squabbling among posters (known as flame wars) and a general dilution in quality had all played a part in the decision to disband it. The more technical posters – the likes of Hal Finney – gravitated to the cryptography mailing list. The more politically and philosophically inclined contributors, it seems, went elsewhere.

How did Satoshi even know about the cryptography list? He must have at least been a lurker, otherwise why would he have gone there? Had he posted on it before, maybe under a different name? Did he know other people who posted on there? There must be some kind of connection.

When he announced Bitcoin on the list, he could have been seeking a critique on it. On the cryptography mailing list he knew he could find a target audience – skilled programmers like Hal Finney – who would understand and even appreciate his project, give him productive, intelligent criticism, and perhaps help develop it. What's more, they would respect his anonymity – Cypherpunks have a long history of communicating anonymously. It is part of their tradition. Pseudonyms, such as Satoshi Nakamoto, are not unusual.

We know Bitcoin required knowledge of Cypherpunk technological ideas: the Hashcash invention of Adam Back and Hal Finney's reusable proofs of work. It's not quite so clear how aware Satoshi was of the work of Wei Dai and Nick Szabo (see the footnote for more on this[92]), although Satoshi did later say, 'Bitcoin is an implementation of Wei Dai's b-money proposal on Cypherpunks...and Nick Szabo's bit gold proposal.'[93]

It all re-enforces this obvious connection between Satoshi and Cypherpunks.

For all the glamour and excitement you might associate with the Cypherpunk world and its revolutionary ideas, there were not many of them. There were even fewer with an interest in developing a new form of digital money. 'Nearly everybody,' says Nick Szabo, 'thought it was a very bad idea. Myself, Wei Dai, and Hal Finney were the only people I know of who liked the idea (or in Dai's case his related idea) enough to pursue it to any significant extent until Nakamoto...Only Finney and Nakamoto were motivated enough to actually implement such a scheme'.[94]

Most libertarians, meanwhile, saw some kind of a return to a gold standard as the answer to the world's monetary woes. Gold is something that Satoshi clearly understood (in amazing detail, in fact, as you're about to find out). The system of mining bitcoins was designed to replicate gold, as was the deliberate deflationary scarcity. But Bitcoin is not gold. The technology – the cryptography – was born somewhere else. So was the anonymity. They were born in the world of Cypherpunks.

As Szabo would later say to me, 'Only a handful of people cared about this kind of thing before Satoshi.'

There really aren't many people who Satoshi could be.

## The Easter eggs that Satoshi left hidden

When some curious souls looked at the code of Bitcoin's genesis block (the first bitcoins that were mined), they found a quotation. It had deliberately been left there, where Satoshi knew people would, sooner or later, find it.

It said: *The Times 03/Jan/2009 Chancellor on brink of second bailout for banks.*

This was the headline from *The Times* – and it came on the

same day the first bitcoins were mined. The UK Chancellor Alistair Darling was bailing out the banks again.

Why did Satoshi write that in?

Satoshi has a habit of letting his statements and his code do more than one job at once. The Bitcoin mining process, for example, disseminates coins but it also maintains the block chain.

The obvious practical reason for the hidden quotation was to add additional verification that those coins were mined on or after that day.

*The Times* was once the world's best-known paper, which makes it an obvious choice. But why not choose *The New York Times*, say?

The main stories in *The New York Times* that day related to Israeli ground offences in the Gaza Strip and what Obama was going to do about the Guantánamo Bay detainees. There was nothing relevant to Bitcoin. By inserting *The Times*, there was now the inference that Bitcoin was some kind of comment on what was happening in the financial markets at the time.

Citing an English paper also re-enforced the British identity he was keen to create in people's minds – rather like the British spelling he used. It added another layer to the disguise.

But that *Times* headline wasn't the only Easter egg he would leave hidden.

When you register on the P2P Foundation, you have to give your birthdate. Satoshi gave April 5th 1975.[95] There might, at first, seem nothing unusual about that.

It's easy to look through history, find some event that took place on April 5th and then attach some kind of significance to it. Pharrell Williams was born that day – perhaps Satoshi was a Pharrell Williams fan and wanted him to sing the theme tune in the Bitcoin movie, should there ever be one.

But, for those who study their money, April 5th was one of the most significant dates in history. On that day in 1933, President Franklin D. Roosevelt signed Executive Order 6102, which made it illegal for American citizens to own gold.

Roosevelt confiscated Americans' gold, gave them dollars in exchange, then de-valued those dollars by 40%, pushing the gold price upwards from $20 to $35. He did this to devalue US debt as a means to deal with the Great Depression – but some say he effectively stole 40% of Americans' wealth.

There are many who regard this action as one of the most unconstitutional things the US government has ever done. It was direct theft by government from the people with no democratic process. While the American constitution clearly states that only gold and silver should be money, suddenly those who owned gold faced imprisonment of five to ten years if they did not hand theirs over to the government.

Perhaps this is too small of a straw to clutch. After all, Satoshi didn't say he was born in the year 1933. He gave the year 1975.

He could have put 1933 as his birthdate – but that would mean he was an unlikely 75 when he designed Bitcoin. 1975 made him a rather more believable 33 in 2008.

So what happened in 1975?

1975 was the year it became legal for American citizens to own gold again.

Such is Satoshi's meticulousness and his knowledge of monetary history, I'm sure this is no coincidence.

By combining the two dates – April 5th and 1975 – he gives himself a credible age *and* manages a dig at what some regard as one of the US government's most unconstitutional actions of the past century.

It's an obscure but brilliant reference. It is also extremely political.

As we'll see, Satoshi was not outspoken in his political beliefs. Then again, Satoshi Nakamoto was just a vehicle to design and develop a product. Judging by the Easter eggs he has left us, the man behind Satoshi, it seems, was rather more political than we realise.

How many people are there who have the knowledge of monetary history to make a reference like that?

Again, the answer is: not many.

Particularly if you confine the search to Cypherpunks.

## The pernicious tax that Satoshi so loathed

Satoshi was remarkably understated in his political pronouncements.

Unlike other, more vocal Cypherpunks, there were no crypto-anarchist manifestos or declarations of the independence of cyberspace.

A currency without government is inherently political, but for the most part he avoided the anti-government rhetoric common among some Bitcoin enthusiasts.

'You will not find a solution to political problems in cryptography,'[96] he was told shortly after proposing Bitcoin. 'Yes,' he replied, 'but we can win a major battle in the arms race and gain a new territory of freedom for several years.'[97] This is pretty strong libertarian stuff – but that was the most extreme comment he would make in the 80,000 words he published online over two years. Most of what he wrote was dedicated to coding.

He did say that Bitcoin is 'very attractive to the libertarian viewpoint if we can explain it properly'[98] – but, again, that was about as far as he went. It was more important to him to get his product right than it was to market it. He would let others do that for him. His product could change the world in a way that his words could not.

In July 2010, when discussing the writing of Bitcoin's Wikipedia entry, he said, 'We don't want to lead with "anonymous (currency)"...(or) "currency outside the reach of any government." I am definitely not making such a taunt or assertion.' He just wanted to briefly explain what Bitcoin did.

This is not just understatement. It was, I am sure, also tactical.

At this early stage he didn't want loud, antagonistic proclamations. It was more important to get Bitcoin working. The more belligerent the tone of the publicity, the more likely it was to invite attack. He needed to get the code as resilient as possible, and Bitcoin widely disseminated and established, before the aggressive attacks came in. The bigger and more established Bitcoin was, the harder it would be to take down.

But he did make one very telling comment on announcing the release of an early version of Bitcoin. Inviting people to try it out, he said, 'Escape the arbitrary inflation risk of centrally managed currencies!'[99]

Inflation – and deflation – are troublesome words that mean different things to different people. This is one of the reasons why there are so many arguments about them. Inflation originally meant the expansion of the supply of money and credit; deflation meant the reduction of the supply of money and credit. But now – to central banks, at least – inflation means rising prices, while deflation means falling prices. To others inflation means government manipulation of money.

Under a fiat money system, inflation – however you define it – of some kind or other is inevitable. Money supply has grown at an average rate of 11.5% per annum since 1989 and will continue to grow as long as lending systems remain as they are. As for rising and falling prices – prices of some things will rise (collectibles, houses in prime areas, stock markets) and others will fall (consumer goods, workers' wages), depending on circumstances. But the broader trend is upwards – CPI has averaged just below 3% since 1989. And of course government manipulation of money of some kind is everywhere and inevitable – it begins with central banks setting interest rates.

Bitcoin is as anti-inflationary an entity as has ever been invented. It was deliberately designed to combat inflation.

First, the supply of bitcoins is clearly scheduled, transparent and finite. 'It is known in advance how many new bitcoins will be created every year...the money supply increases by a planned amount,' says Satoshi.[100] We know the maximum number of bitcoins will be 21 million.

As for rising or falling prices, if more people start using bitcoins at a faster rate than they are mined, then prices of things, measured in bitcoins, will fall. This is the dynamic we have seen so far – as the price of a coin has risen from pennies to hundreds of dollars, the relative price of goods has fallen.

If the reverse happens – and Bitcoin sees fewer users – then prices of goods will rise.

This system does dramatically favour early adopters, which is why there are so many rags-to-riches stories. Pyramid and Ponzi schemes share this trait. But, as Satoshi says, 'Coins have to get initially distributed somehow, and a constant rate seems like the best formula.'[101] (And I'll bet that for all the people who have made millions, there are many times more early-adopters kicking themselves for selling too soon.)

Finally, of course, as an open-source currency with no central issuer, Bitcoin is outside government purview. Governments can't issue bitcoins. They can't declare what bitcoin interest rates are. They can't manipulate bitcoin inflation statistics. So, Bitcoin is anti-inflation – however you define it and whatever form it takes.

We have another clue, then, about Satoshi. He hated inflation.

Bitcoin is 'more typical of a precious metal,' Satoshi says. 'Instead of the supply changing to keep the value the same, the supply is predetermined and the value changes. As the number of users grows, the value per coin increases.'[102]

Satoshi was a bit of a gold bug as well, then.

## He might have coded the new money system of the world, but he didn't have much of a computer

Let's look for a moment at some of the things we know for sure.

We'll start with his computer.

Satoshi used Windows. Windows is the most common

computer operating system in the world: nothing remarkable there. Bitcoin was compiled using Microsoft Visual Studio.

What is remarkable is that the original Bitcoin code was not multi-platform – it was Windows only. That is unusual for a high-level coder; they usually prefer Linux or Macs.

Steve Jobs will be turning in his grave, but Satoshi did not have a Mac. He always had to ask others – usually the 10,000-bitcoin-pizza-buyer Laszlo – to test the system on Macs and would rely on them to make it work. 'Good, so I take it that's a confirmation that it's working on Mac as well,' he said when a new bit of tech was being tried out.[103]

Despite having a Windows machine, we also know Satoshi did not have an Intel Core i5 processor or an AMD processor. He said, 'I hope someone can test an i5 or AMD to check that I built it right. I don't have either to test with.'[104]

But by August 2010 he *was* using the operating system Linux. He says, 'I could only get this working with Linux'.[105]

We also know he was using the operating system GNU,[106] and he used Open Office to write the Bitcoin white paper. It is interesting how he favoured open-source software in both cases.

It's also worth noting that his computer might not have been top drawer. Though one theory says he was running a powerful 64-core cluster, another says the opposite. At Bit-coinTalk, Moonshadow writes: 'it's pretty obvious that his machine wasn't particularly powerful, as in the very beginning (looking at the charts from blockexployer) it would take hours between blocks...even at the minimum difficulty of 1.'[107]

Satoshi might have programmed the new money system of the world, but he didn't have much of a computer.

# Where in the world is Satoshi?

What about where Satoshi lives – any clues there?

Yes – he left two clues.

First, the times when he used to post online.

Over the two years that Satoshi posted, he was most active between the hours of 3pm and 2am Greenwich Mean Time (GMT), according to a survey put together by Stefan Thomas, a Swiss computer scientist. After 3am GMT posting was light and there was barely an entry in the six hours between 5am and 11am. Then from 11am to 3pm posting would start gradually increasing again. This pattern was consistent during the week and at weekends.

The first observation here is that he maintained regular hours – unusual for a computer hacker. We can come to a tentative conclusion here. On the basis that young men tend to keep more irregular hours, this also suggests someone who is older than, say, 30, rather than younger.

The next observation is that Satoshi's posts were time-stamped at GMT. (He would have known how to change this setting, if he wanted.) People wrongly assume GMT is UK local time, when in fact it is only so for the five months of the year between October and March – for the rest of the time the UK is an hour ahead of GMT. It appears to me that the use of GMT was just another, slightly erroneous, part of the British disguise.

Then we must ask – what was he doing in the time that his posting disappeared – in the hours between 5am and 11am GMT? Perhaps he was in an environment where he couldn't post – at school or at work, maybe, but the more likely explanation is that that was when he slept. In the 'low-posting' hours on either side, he was either going to sleep or waking up.

But if he was in the UK, 5/6am to 11/12am is a rather odd time to sleep.

But 5am to 11am GMT equates to 1am to 7am Eastern Standard Time (EST) or 10pm to 4am Pacific Standard Time (PST).

There are numerous ways to interpret the data. The obvious interpretation is that he was based in the EST zone and kept normal working and sleeping hours. Activity would peter out at around ten at night and start to pick up at nine or ten the following morning, with peak activity being between the normal working hours of 9am and 6pm.

And, of course, there are a number of people in other time zones – particularly on the West coast of the US – who keep EST working hours.

There was another clue.

After an early crash in January 2009 when just Satoshi and Finney were mining, Finney posted a very detailed log of debugging information.[108]

It showed Satoshi was running a computer in California.

The next time there was a crash, Satoshi asked for the log to be emailed to him privately, off-list. Was he protecting information about his whereabouts?

# The name that is no more real than Elton John or Michael Caine

At first, everyone took Satoshi at face value.

'I thought I was dealing with a young man of Japanese ancestry who was very smart and sincere,'[109] said Finney.

'It didn't occur to me that he was anonymous or that it was a pseudonym at the time,' Adam Back remarked about Satoshi's early emails to him.

There are not many Satoshi Nakamotos in the world.

There was a Satoshi Nakamoto in Japan. He died in 2010. He was a concrete expert.

There was also a Satoshi Nakamoto in Honolulu. He died in 2008. (There's also an NSA station there, which has added to the theory that Bitcoin is actually the NSA and that the name was actually a tribute to a brilliant, dead, secret Japanese-American code-breaker.)

And there was *Newsweek*'s Dorian Satoshi Nakamoto, who thought Bitcoin was called 'Bitcom'.

A quick search on LinkedIn reveals some other living Satoshi Nakamotos (and a load of bogus ones) but none fit the profile even remotely. This implies that it's a pseudonym – and this would tie in with the Cypherpunk traditions of anonymity.

But perhaps Satoshi has left us some Easter eggs in his name. Many people have pored over it looking for clues.

One poster by the name of jackofspades discovered short-ened versions of leading tech companies – SAmsung, TOSHIba, NAKaminchi, Apple and MOTOrola – to make SA TOSHI NAK A MOTO.

Others have found meaning in the Japanese. Satoshi is a Japanese boy's name. It means 'clear-thinking', 'quick-witted' or 'wise'. 'Naka' has various meanings – 'medium', 'inside', or 'relationship', while 'moto' means 'origins' or 'foundation'. So his name might mean something like 'wise relationship origin', for example.

There is always the possibility that Satoshi Nakamoto

might just have been chosen, like Elton John or Michael Caine, because it sounded good.

Then there are the initials – S and N – do they have any significance? We'll come back to them.

What about the registration of the website? Are there any clues there?

Bitcoin.org was registered through the website AnonymousSpeech, which declares it 'will not respond to inquiries made by foreign governments or private parties...Any inquiries regarding the identity of our subscribers are ignored. **We do not respond to any of them.**'[110]

Nothing to be found there.

It was registered to the following address: 133 Sakura House Nakano-ku Tokyo-to 164-0011.

There is no such address.

Sakura House is a chain of guesthouses in Tokyo – indeed Sakura is a common girls' name. The Tokyo postcode 164-0011 is just down the road from Nakano station.

So, despite there being no such address, there is some real-world knowledge behind it.

I tried calling the registered number – +50.55396801 – with the Japanese dialling code +81. No such number exists – no surprise there.

There is no country with the code +50 either. The code +505 is Nicaragua. When I tried calling that number in Nicaragua, I again found no such number exists.

As late as 2011, there were still no Japanese translations of the primary documents or of the Bitcoin website. Even the address 'bitcoin.jp' (the Japanese version of bitcoin.org) was not registered until 2011, when Mike Caldwell claimed it – and he definitely isn't Japanese.

There is some affinity with Japan: the name and the website registration address. But my conclusion is that, in the search for Satoshi, Japan is a red herring.

And, if he is Japanese, he doesn't half speak good English.

## What nationality is Satoshi?

In the three years Satoshi was active online he wrote over 80,000 words.

There is barely a typo. He's a more consistent writer than me and I'm supposed to be a professional.

On one occasion he said, 'a obvious' instead of 'an obvious'. On another he said 'adminning' instead of 'administering'.[111] (But this is acceptable coders' abbreviation.)

There is just one spelling mistake – 'idealogical' instead of 'ideological'[112] – an easy mistake to make. (If I could find 'idealogical' in the writings of one of the suspects, I might have a lead.)

This is someone that is not just meticulous, but a practised and accomplished writer. It does not necessarily mean he has published books, but I would have thought he must at least have been active either in academic circles or on the blogosphere, or both. It does not necessarily mean his mother tongue was English, but it is indicative of considerable time spent in an English-speaking country.

His style is calm, logical, unflustered, measured, careful and scientific. It is not flowery or emotional in any way. His writing can take some understanding at times on my part, but that is because the subjects he wrote about – computer code – are often alien to me. Those that the writing was intended for understood him.

There were just one or two exclamation marks – a 'Thanks guys!' or a 'Hurray!' (unusual, though not incorrect, spelling of hooray) when a bug was fixed.

His language is often colloquial. He uses common internet parlance – expressions like 'sweet', '+1', 'kinda' and 'OP'. 'WTF?' he declares, 'How did we get on that? AFAIK, the only e-mail is if you tell the forum to do notifications, and I guess the wiki registration'.[113] By the way, the phrase 'do notifications' is American; the British would tend to say 'make notifications'.

Satoshi tends to use British spellings – so the American 'labor' or 'flavor' will be 'labour' and 'flavour'; the American 'modernize' or 'formalize' will be 'modernise' and 'formalise'[114] – although he is inconsistent in this regard. For example, 'decentralized' is sometimes spelt with a 'z'. In UK English, either is acceptable.

Several times he refers to a 'mobile' rather than the American 'cell phone'. For example, 'The cash register displays a QR-code encoding a bitcoin address and amount on a screen and you photo it with your mobile.'[115]

He says 'maths' not the American 'math'.[116] He refers to 'flats' rather than 'apartments'.[117]

Consider the following quote from Satoshi: 'Sorry to be a wet blanket. Writing a description for (Bitcoin) for general audiences is bloody hard. There's nothing to relate it to.'[118]

The use of 'bloody' as an expletive is common in Britain, Australia and even parts of Canada, but it is not so common in the United States, except among Anglophiles. According to the Oxford English Dictionary, the use of word 'bloody' as an expletive, 'spread to most other parts of the English-speaking world, with the notable exception of the United

States, where it has apparently only ever achieved limited currency'.

Finally there is that reference to the English newspaper, *The Times*, in the code of the first block of bitcoins that were mined.

This all places him on the European side of the Atlantic – unless this was a deliberate trick to throw people.

It might well have been.

The American blogger Gwern writes, 'It's perfectly easy to pick up Briticisms if you watch BBC programs or read *The Economist* or *Financial Times* (I do all three and as it happens, I use "bloody" all the time in colloquial speech – a check of my IRC logs shows me using it 72 times, and at least once in my more formal writings on gwern.net, and "mobile phone" pops up 3 or 4 times in my chat logs; yet I have spent perhaps 3 days in the UK in my life.'[119]

In other words, the British spelling – like the Japanese name and perhaps even the German email address – might be another red herring.

In one of his early replies on the cryptography mailing list, Satoshi wrote the following: 'The send dialog is re-size-able and you can enter as long of a message as you like'.[120] We see a definite non-English-ism – 'as long of a message'. The phrasing is also common in the US and Ireland, but not in the UK.

Satoshi often describes things as 'neat'.[121] That is common in the US. It is rare in Britain and Ireland.

He mentions 'pocket change'. Again that is not an expression you hear this side of the Atlantic – but one that you do hear in the US.

Satoshi refers to 'heating oil'.[122] The expression is also uncommon in the UK, where most homes are heated with gas. When referring to heating oil, we tend to call it paraffin. Again, that places him on the American side of the Atlantic.

Another observation: at one point Satoshi says he is 'Not sure what it should be named.'[123] An Englishman might say, 'not sure what it should be called'.

This all indicates, contrarily, that his English was learnt on the other side of the Atlantic. Confusing. It might be, of course, that he learnt his English on both sides of the Atlantic.

There is one final quirk that I've noticed. Satoshi says, 'At some point I became convinced there was a way to do this without any trust required at all and couldn't resist to keep thinking about it'.[124]

The use of the word 'to' stood out for me – 'couldn't resist to keep thinking about it'. That does not sound like a native English speaker. I would say, 'I couldn't resist thinking about it' or 'I couldn't stop thinking about it'. The use of the 'to keep' sounds foreign to me – like somebody translating literally from one of the Latin, Germanic or Scandinavian languages.

But this is one small thing in 80,000 words or more. It probably means nothing.

The words are disappointingly inconclusive. But the punctuation is much more intriguing.

## The curious case of the spaces after full stops

My publisher, Dan Kieran, says that if he reads manuscripts that have been submitted to him with two spaces after a full stop, he knows the author has not had books published before, because two spaces are no longer used in print. Typographers and just about every widely used style guide seem to agree on this.

The practice of using two spaces seems to have been born because of the shortcomings of early printers. Two spaces were used to make the break from the previous sentence clear. Those who learnt to type on typewriters would have been taught to use double spacing for this reason. As space came to have more of a premium in printed media, and with the improved clarity of modern printing, the convention of single-spacing took over.

The practice of double-spacing is known as 'English spacing' – single spacing is known as 'French spacing'. Ironically, English spacing seems to be more common in America – particularly in academic circles.

But here is an interesting contradiction that nobody has picked up.

In his Bitcoin white paper (November 2008), in his posts on the cryptography mailing list (January 2009), on Sourceforge (January 2009 to December 2010) and in his posts on the Bitcoin forum (November 2009 to December 2010) Satoshi uses two spaces after each full stop.

But in his announcement of Bitcoin to the P2P Foundation (February 2009), and in the subsequent discussion there, he only uses one space after each full stop.[125]

It is possible that the P2P forum software used to collapse double-spacing if you cut and paste. But I found this was not the case when I tried it out more recently.

What can we deduce from this?

Assuming the P2P software hasn't compressed his

spacing, the first possibility is that that the P2P Foundation announcement was written by someone else.

Another is that Satoshi submitted his white paper with the correct, academic English spacing, while his announcement to the P2P Foundation with the non-academic single-spacing was appropriate for that circle. In other words, he was aware of both conventions.

But in that case he should have continued using single spacing. He didn't. Elsewhere, he went back to double. Perhaps the spaces-after-full-stops side of Satoshi's persona was not yet fully formed.

As I study the rest of Satoshi's punctuation in search of clues, I find that it, like his English, is consistent and uncomplicated.

There is the occasional loose apostrophe. He writes 90's, rather than 90s or '90s – but (though grammatically incorrect) this is generally accepted as it's so common.

He uses double inverted commas or speech marks. These are more common in the US, Canada, Australia and continental Europe, while single quotation marks are more common in the UK and South Africa.

Finally, his use of the hyphen: good but not impeccable. He will use it when two or more words are put together to make an adjective – 'it is a piece of open-source software', for example. But long-term future is 'long term future', pseudo-code is 'pseudocode', account-based commands becomes 'account based commands'.

# Why Bitcoin is not a product of youth or old age, but of middle age

There is something we can learn from his double-spacing.

I was born in 1969. The first word-processors were coming out in the mid-1980s, when I was in my teens, and I learnt to type on them. Despite going to an academic school, I never even knew about double-spacing. However, my mother, who learnt to type on a typewriter, practised this convention and insists on it even now.

So, Satoshi's double spacing suggests someone who is a little older – probably born before 1975 – when he says he was born.[126] There are plenty of academic coders younger than that who write with two spaces – so this is not conclusive.

But Bitcoin isn't a product of youth like Facebook, Twitter or Snapchat. It's not enough to be a whizz on computers. It requires knowledge of so many other areas, which would have taken years to accumulate. The language in which Bitcoin is written – C++ – is also regarded by coders as 'old school'.

All in all, I dismiss the idea that Satoshi was in his twenties when he created Bitcoin.

On the other hand, I cannot see that he was born before that key period of 1955–56 – i.e. older than 54 in 2009. He would have missed the computer revolution and been too old to learn the code he would have needed. What's more, ambition fades with age. Much older than that and he would have lacked the drive.

Martti Malmi tells me, 'I feel like he is maybe in his 30s or 40s, I've never met him – nobody's ever met him – by the name Satoshi of course – all my contact with him was by email and in the forums.'

I'm inclined to agree. I suggest he was born somewhere between 1955 and 1975 – most probably between 1960 and 1970.

## How rich is Satoshi?

Satoshi says he had been coding Bitcoin for some 18 months before announcing it in January 2009.[127] He would then spend another two years working on it publicly before he left the Bitcoin forums in December 2010, and at least another few months working with core developers after that.

Even if he lived the most frugal of lifestyles, over four years working on the project without pay suggests he must have had some other form of income. Perhaps he came from a rich family, or he had some kind of grant, fellowship or sponsorship. Perhaps he had another job or freelanced. Speculation aside, he must have had some other form of income or capital to draw on. I believe that it was a significant figure – enough to give him the confidence to begin work on a project that could last any number of years without any guarantee of return at the end.

A coder and independent security researcher named Sergio Lerner conducted a detailed analysis of the block chain at the time Satoshi was still mining. He concluded that Satoshi had mined at least one million bitcoins – more precisely 1,148,800. Lerner felt that if any of these coins had been spent, it would not be difficult to work out Satoshi's identity – the recipient of the coins would know, unless the sender had sent the coins anonymously. But it appears that none of them were ever spent.

My own basic analysis shows that of the 1,624,250 bitcoins that were mined by December 31st 2009 with the completion of block 32485, only 27% have been moved. Somebody – or bodies – in the small circle of early miners has kept around 1.2 million.

It is, of course, yet another gold star to Satoshi. He was aware of Bitcoin's lack of anonymity (he had sacrificed it in order to improve its performance and reduce bandwidth needed), so even here he left no clues.

But that also means, using a $500 bitcoin price, that there is a fortune worth over half a billion dollars he has left untouched.

It would take someone with extraordinary willpower, which we know Satoshi has, not to spend a penny of that. An amazing fortune, many years in the making, taking genius, application, good fortune and everything else you need to have uncommon success – and he barely touches a penny of it.

If Satoshi was very poor, I do not believe such levels of willpower would be possible. The more comfortably off he is, the more likely it is he would be able to resist the temptation to dip into his fortune.

It all makes me think that Satoshi had money.

However, he may not have a particularly powerful computer – which suggests he did not have *that much* money. Yet another contradiction.

In addition, his use of AnonymousSpeech to register and host the Bitcoin domain was not cheap. It would have cost about a $1,000 for a service he could have had elsewhere, but less anonymously, for about $50.

The inference is that he did not invent Bitcoin for the

money, nor does he particularly value the things many of us lesser mortals might spend our fortunes on – houses, cars and gorgeous watches. But if he did have money, how did he come by it? Was it perhaps for some other coding work he had done in the past? Such work can be very well paid.

Whether as a writer or coder or something else, I'm convinced there must be examples of Satoshi's other work on the internet. Is he hiding in plain view?

## The one-man-band who was an old-school coder

On top of everything else, Satoshi was, as Gavin Andresen, says a 'brilliant programmer'.[128]

'When there was a problem with the protocol,' says Martti Malmi to me, 'he fixed it in one day or something like that, when it would take someone else weeks. If he is just one person, he did an amazing job with the code.'

It seems he was just one person. Teams tend to leave notes for each other explaining why they've done certain things. There were none of these in Bitcoin, only notes to self. The consistency of style also indicates the coding of one man working alone. It seems, until a few months before he left, 'almost all modifications to the source code were done by Satoshi – he accepted contributions relatively rarely'.[129]

The actual codebase was not so sophisticated from the point of view of software engineering principles. It was 'both elegant and inelegant, written neither by a total amateur or a professional programmer'.[130] What was exceptional was its robustness.

Coders all agree that a huge amount of work went into it. 'Satoshi was working on this idea for quite a while,' said one coder. 'I don't think this was something he threw together in a couple of months...He may have been working on it for several years. He took great pains to ensure it was sufficiently evolved such that it wouldn't simply die shortly after its release.'[131]

Italian coder Alessandro Polverini tells me in an email, 'He created the initial work to let the community verify that the idea was sound and functional, and then left to the community the burden of evolving and improving it, of making it more modular and documented. Some of the people he left it to are very, very competent and skilled.'

There are hundreds of different programming languages, but Satoshi chose to code in C++.

In C++, programmers have to do things for themselves that are automated in later languages – they are working with 'nuts and bolts', close to the hardware of the computer. This means there are many who don't go near C++, finding it too complicated, though it remains popular with games designers – and cryptographers. Other coders, such as Wei Dai, think it is 'a pretty standard choice for anyone wanting to build such a piece of software'.[132] C++ is a computing subculture in itself.

Dan Kaminsky – the hacker who tried to crack Bitcoin – was initially dismissive about the choice to use C++. He thought it was a weakness. His attempts to hack Bitcoin changed his mind: 'in the context of actual security paranoia, C++ *is* actually a great choice. It allows for clean infrastructure, and if you know what you're doing, *you actually know what you're doing*. Modern languages like JavaScript and Ruby are great, in that they do a huge amount for you under the surface, but then you don't actually know what they're going to do.'[133]

So, C++ offers little by the way of shortcuts, but it also offers more control and predictability. You are not relying on other people's code. Instead you are 'close to the metal'. So, C++ might have been chosen for its resilience. But it is also the obvious – if not the only – choice for a Windows programmer like Satoshi.

Hal Finney said it's 'hard to master C++ if you didn't learn it while you're young'.[134] A veteran programmer, who preferred to remain anonymous, said to me, 'C++ is somewhat unique. Mastering it is very time-consuming and, while many programmers have some familiarity with it, I believe it's becoming increasingly rare for one to truly be proficient in it as Satoshi undoubtedly is.' Moreover the Bitcoin code doesn't 'have the more modern style of current expert C++ programmers'. A younger coder might have chosen Java, Ruby or Python, but even if they chose C++, the style would be more modern.

So Satoshi was not a young man – and he learnt his coding craft a while back.

But merely knowing C++ is a far cry from being a world-class programmer. 'Whoever coded Bitcoin', says my anonymous veteran programmer, 'was an expert C++ coder.' To reach that level of competence would require a '5–10 year obsession'. And, as Wei Dai notes, 'to have implemented Bitcoin (and to do it securely to boot)' their programming skills would have to have been 'kept sharp'.[135]

This immediately rules out many Satoshi candidates.

Hal Finney does not code in C++ but in C.

Adam Back also too favours C – and his coding style is

'wildly different', says one of my coder sleuths. Back himself tells me, 'I did know C++ about 15 years back. I prefer C. I just think C++ is unhelpfully complex.' (See the footnote for more on why Back is not Satoshi.[136])

Which prominent Cypherpunk had not only the interest, but also the specific C++ coding skills to develop Bitcoin?

I returned to my anonymous veteran programmer. We were looking at the C++ code of prominent Cypherpunks. With Finney and Back ruled out, he says, 'I looked at Ben Laurie, Zooko, and even Richard Clayton and came up with nothing interesting'.

But there was one obvious candidate.

Wei Dai.

He's an academic. He was a Cypherpunk. His b-money paper actually describes the ledger that would become the Bitcoin block chain. He had the interest. He's supremely intelligent. He is a Windows Visual C++ programmer. And he even has a C++ library, which Satoshi used.

The vet says to me, 'Wei Dai's Crypto++ library is written in C++. It contains implementations of all the cryptographic primitives required to build Bitcoin and a deep familiarity with most of them would be required...the original bitcoin lifted the SHA256 implementation directly from Wei's library. Both codebases targeted Windows and even the structure of both projects is very similar. And then you have b-money...I challenge you to even find one other Cypherpunk who writes C++ at that level.'

Have I found my man, at last?

Nope.

Satoshi actually emailed Dai prior to Bitcoin's release.

'I was very interested to read your b-money page,' he said.

'I'm getting ready to release a paper that expands on your ideas into a complete working system. Adam Back (Hashcash.org) noticed the similarities and pointed me to your site.'[137]

Dai has shown me the emails. I doubt Satoshi would have faked a correspondence with an alter ego before the paper had even been published – and then shared it with people like me.

I then found these remarks by Wei Dai in the comments section of a blog discussing how to make money by mining bitcoins.

'I didn't create Bitcoin,' he says, 'but only described a similar idea more than a decade ago. And my understanding is that the creator of Bitcoin, who goes by the name Satoshi Nakamoto, didn't even read my article before reinventing the idea himself. He learned about it afterward and credited me in his paper. So my connection with the project is quite limited.'[138] Wei Dai went on – with rather more enthusiasm – to describe how he had just started mining coins.

This could all be an elaborate ruse to throw people off the scent, so I had three different coders compare Satoshi's code with Dai's. They might be coding in the same language, but the style is different.

It's pretty clear that Wei Dai is not Satoshi.

I'm starting to think that the whole Cypherpunk theme might be another huge red herring. As Wei Dai says, 'My guess is that he's not anyone who was previously active in the academic cryptography or Cypherpunk communities, because otherwise he probably would have been identified by now based on his writing and coding styles.'

But there is one last Cypherpunk possibility.

# Uncovering Satoshi Nakamoto: the real man behind Bitcoin

*(N.B. There are many other names that have been put forward as possible Satoshis. I address all those who have not so far been mentioned in Appendix II.)*

Of all those on whose shoulders Bitcoin is standing, there is one man who ticks an uncanny number of boxes.

He's a shy, retiring computer coder based in California. He's been heavily involved in digital cash systems almost all his working life. He is an intellectual heavyweight and polymath. And his knowledge of money is second to none.

Everything about his work screams, 'Bitcoin!'

This man is Nick Szabo.

But there is one crucial issue: every bit of evidence that suggests he's Satoshi is circumstantial.

Born in 1964, Szabo graduated from the University of Washington in 1989 with a degree in computer science.[139] In 2006 he was awarded a professional degree (Juris Doctor) in law from George Washington University. We have a computer scientist and a postgraduate, born smack in the middle of my ideal target age range (between 1960 and 1970).

Szabo was a Cypherpunk. As early as 1993 he was active on the Cypherpunks mailing list. Another box ticked.

Even then he was obsessed with the idea of digital cash. 'The future of Cypherpunks' goals,' he wrote in 1993, is 'most obviously digital cash'.[140] It is a theme which would never leave his work.

He is a veritable polymath. The array of papers and essays he has written on his blog, Unenumerated, and on his website (szabo.best.vwh.net) is breathtaking. Here are just some

of the subjects he covered: ecommerce, commodity speculation, internet security, mining the ocean beds, the hourglass,
micropayments, insurance, smart contracts, law, distributed
systems, financial engineering, software architecture, technology product management, algorithmic information
theory, intrapolynomial cryptography, gold, politics, even
the United States Constitution.

But the subjects that he returns to most are money,
money systems and smart contracts. In this area, his knowledge is deeper than almost anyone's.

His 2002 paper, *Shelling Out: The Origins of Money*,[141] is,
as he himself says, 'almost essential reading' if you want to
understand Bitcoin. Central to Szabo's theory on money is
that it emerged from collectibles (valuable jewellery and so
on), which have a cost of production to them. 'Collectible' is
an unusual word both he and Satoshi (bitcoins are 'more like
a collectible or commodity'[142] he said) use repeatedly – and
we already know about Bitcoin's cost of production. He also
seems to have been a bit of a gold bug.

His academic brilliance at the intersection of money,
computer science, law, economics and, of course, Cypherpunk means he is one of the few people in the world, perhaps
the only person, with the breadth, depth and specificity of
knowledge to design Bitcoin.

## He has a deep understanding of anonymity, he designed the precursor to Bitcoin and he has the same writing style

In the late 1990s and throughout the 2000s Szabo would propose and develop his idea for bit gold. It's uncannily similar to Bitcoin, even in name.

He says, for example, 'The basic idea of bit gold is for "bit gold miners" to set their computers to solving computationally intensive mathematical puzzles, then to publish the solutions to these puzzles in secure public registries, giving them unique title to these provably scarce and securely time-stamped bits...bit gold will be entirely public: no one gains secure title to any puzzle solutions until they are published.'[143] If that's not Bitcoin in a nutshell, I'll eat my hat.

I found this from him, written back in 1993 to the Cypherpunks:

In my limited experience creating Internet pseudonyms, I've been quite distracted by the continual need to avoid leaving pointers to my True Name lying around – excess mail to/from my True Name, shared files, common peculiarities (eg misspellings in written text), traceable logins, etc...All kinds of security controls – crypto, access, information, inference – have to be continually on my mind when using pseudonymous accounts. The hazards are everywhere. With our current tools it's practically impossible to maintain an active pseudonym for a long period of time against a sufficiently determined opponent, and quite a hassle to maintain even a modicum of decent security.[144]

This shows a deep understanding of what is required to stay

anonymous. Fifteen years after writing this post, he might have mastered the art.

Despite publishing a blog and copies of all his papers online, I could find just one photograph of him on the internet – a still from a 1997 video, which I found on Twitter. Information about his private life is scarce.

One glance at his blog shows he's an accomplished and practised writer, both online and in academia. We have another box ticked.

What's more, Satoshi and Szabo's writing styles are similar. I am not the first person to observe this. An anonymous blogger by the name of Skye Grey has posted two blog entries[145] in which he drew the same conclusion, saying, 'analysis of the content-neutral expressions found in the Bitcoin whitepaper indicates a match with NS's writing tics, at a level that only has a one in a thousand chance to be a coincidence'.[146] Others – the blogger Gwern, in particular – have debunked Grey's methodology[147] and its 'one in a thousand' conclusion, but there are still commonalities.

Grey tends to focus on Szabo's use of particular words and phrases. 'Trusted third party' is one such unusual expression that both often use, 'shenanigans' is another. (Szabo even wrote a paper in 2001 called 'Trusted Third Parties Are Security Holes'.)

I've also noticed some similarities in their punctuation. Their use of the hyphen, for example (good but not perfect) and of bullet points is similar. They both use the same double inverted commas as speech marks. They both write '90's' with an apostrophe, rather than '90s'.

There is also the curious issue of the spaces after full stops. In his early work Szabo used to use English spacing

– two spaces after a full stop. In his later work, he switched to one. So he was aware of both conventions. Indeed, in an email to me, written in haste, Szabo used both French and English spacing. That is another box ticked.

Of course, there are many aspects of their writing that are different. Szabo does not use British spelling. He does not use British expressions like mobile phone, flat and bloody. There is a lot more humour to his work than Satoshi's. He spells 'ideological' correctly. His sentences are longer. These can all be explained.

Szabo has extensive knowledge of Britain and British history (gained while developing his legal and money theories). It's not so hard to affect British-isms. The sole purpose of the Satoshi persona was to develop Bitcoin – why would he crack jokes? As for the spelling mistake – they happen sometimes. One in 80,000 words is forgivable.

Stylometrics expert John Noecker Jr. analysed some of Nick Szabo's work for me, having already run tests on the writing of Satoshi and various others. He tells me:

> In July of last year we found that Neil King [following a Fast Company article, King was thought to be Satoshi[148]] was a pretty good stylistic match, but it wasn't close enough to make any kind of real call. So we just stop working on it. Then we looked at Hal Finney and Nick Szabo. What we found was that Nick Szabo was a much closer match. He is a better candidate than King in every single experiment that we did. Normally we see like a mixture for example King was the best in 80% and then we would get some other

candidate that came through, so that is quite conclusive. In this Hal Finney or Nick Szabo are always the top performer.

So, stylistically, Nick Szabo *and* Hal Finney are the closest matches. Many, including me, have given great credence to the idea that Szabo did the writing and Finney did the coding – that Satoshi is Nick Szabo *and* Hal Finney. But we know now that Finney was not Satoshi.

The similarities in their writing styles are no surprise. Their areas of interest are similar, of course, but Finney was also something of a mentor to Szabo. They had known each other since the early 90s and, with some searching, you can find conversations between the two on archived Cypherpunk mailing lists. There is more to the Szabo-Finney-Satoshi relationship than is openly stated.

When Satoshi wrote to Dai, he was excited that Finney had given him a 'high-level overview,' which he then quoted in full.[149] Remember, Finney was the first to reply to Satoshi's announcements. Finney was the one with high price projections, it was his critique and, more importantly, his coding abilities that Satoshi wanted to access when he went to the cryptography mailing list in the first place and it was he who would mine the first coins after Satoshi, debug the system and become one of the first developers.

So, back to Szabo's writing.

In the spring of 2014, students and researchers from Aston University ran linguistic tests on the Bitcoin white paper against the writing of 11 different authors. They also concluded that Szabo was probably the author.[150]

There is plenty more yet.

Like Satoshi, Szabo had a Windows machine – a 2004 slide show[151] posted on Szabo's site was put together in Windows. Another box ticked.

George Washington University in Washington DC, where Szabo studied for his law degree, is based in the EST zone. That would fit his work-sleep schedule, but he is actually based in California. In the PST zone, it is definitely conceivable he kept the hours that he did (he is an early riser). More importantly, it is where the computer that Satoshi used to mine coins is located. We have another box ticked.

A small thing: both Szabo and Satoshi reference economist Carl Menger in their discussions about money.

Then, what for me is a humdinger: Szabo actually *worked* for Chaum's Digicash in the 1990s[152] – so he had hands-on experience. I even found his old Digicash email address. He also wrote a paper on Chaum's groundbreaking blind signatures technology and how digital cash works.[153]

## When timing is everything

Satoshi says he had been working on Bitcoin for 18 months prior to 2009. This takes us back to 2007, when Szabo had just completed his law degree. There was room in his life for another big project.

Indeed, in spring 2008, Szabo was actively looking for work. He wrote on his blog, 'I am now publicly offering my consulting services. Besides topics I regularly blog about, my expertise includes technology product management (especially for e-commerce and wireless products and services), smart contracts, financial engineering, software architecture and engineering, and computer/network security. I can travel just about anywhere.'[154] All of these, incidentally, are areas of expertise Bitcoin's inventor would have needed.

The circumstantial evidence continues.

In April 2008, Szabo wrote on his blog about bit gold, 'I suspect this is all obscure enough that (a) it may require most people to sit down and work it out for themselves carefully before it can be well understood, and (b) it would greatly benefit from a demonstration, an experimental market (with e.g. a trusted third party substituted for the complex security that would be needed for a real system)'. This echoes Satoshi's concern that explaining Bitcoin to people is 'bloody hard',[155] but more important was Szabo's next remark. 'Anybody want to help me code one up?'

This came just at the point when Szabo was looking for work – when he had a gap in his life.

Four months after asking for 'help coding one up' the website bitcoin.org was registered. Four months later it was mentioned on the cryptography mailing list. Another two months after that, the first coins were mined. This was a ten-month period. It could just be coincidence, of course. But the timing is right.

It's worth stressing that Bitcoin's original release was 14,500 lines of, as described to me, 'messy greenfield C++ code'. It's not a trivial amount of code – but it's achievable in this ten-month period. Perhaps it didn't take as long as the 18 months Satoshi said it did.

There was another bit of unusual timing.

Just three days before Satoshi mined the first ever bitcoins and announced his creation, Szabo was on his site revising his 2005 and 2008 posts about bit gold. I managed to find the originals[156] in an old archive and compared it to the tidied-up versions. Only typos were modified. Why would he suddenly make those modifications then? Why would you go back and edit that particular three-year-old blog entry?

I did find another example of a modified post.[157] The post was from November 2005, but it was modified in August 2008 – at the same time bitcoin.org was registered. The subject of the post was private and abstract money.

Then, a week after bitcoin.org was registered, Szabo wrote on his blog:

> The unforgeable costliness pattern includes the following basic steps:
>
> (1) find or create a class of objects that is highly improbable, takes much effort to make, or both, and such that the measure of their costliness can be verified by other parties.
>
> (2) use the objects to enable a protocol or institution to cross trust boundaries
>
> There are some problems involved with implementing unforgeable costliness on a computer. If such problems can be overcome, we can achieve bit gold. This would be the first online currency based on highly distributed trust and unforgeable costliness rather than trust in a single entity and traditional accounting controls.[158]

Again, the similarities are uncanny.

Between October 2008 and April 2009, the period when Bitcoin was first released into the open-source community,

Szabo's blog ceased to be updated. There were only 're-runs' as Szabo called them.

What was he doing that was taking up his time?

## The breach of trust that inspired Bitcoin

'The root problem with conventional currency is all the trust that's required to make it work',[159] said Satoshi when he announced Bitcoin to the P2P foundation.

On his blog Nick Szabo wrote, 'The problem, in a nutshell, is that our money currently depends on trust in a third party for its value.'[160]

He continued, 'all money mankind has ever used has been insecure in one way or another. This insecurity has been manifested in a wide variety of ways, from counterfeiting to theft, but the most pernicious of which has probably been inflation...Bit gold may provide us with a money of unprecedented security from these dangers.'[161] Satoshi echoed him: 'The central bank must be trusted not to debase the currency, but the history of fiat currencies is full of breaches of that trust. Banks must be trusted to hold our money and transfer it electronically, but they lend it out in waves of credit bubbles with barely a fraction in reserve. We have to trust them with our privacy, trust them not to let identity thieves drain our accounts...With e-currency based on cryptographic proof, without the need to trust a third party middleman, money can be secure.'[162]

In his younger days on the Cypherpunks mailing list, Szabo was outspoken and strongly libertarian. He used to attend libertarian meetings in the early 1990s. On his website he has a link to famous Ronald Reagan quotes. He seemed to soften a little with age, but from 2007 he began to grow vocal again. He wrote a piece, entitled 'Ten ways to make a political difference'.[163] Most importantly, 'Be prepared to vote with your feet,' he suggested. 'Add interstate and international diversity to your personal and business networks' so that if you want to move somewhere else, 'the exit costs will be low...Grow interpolitical roots so that no single polity can chop down your tree'.

He argued that you should serve on a jury to influence the law in action. He recommended making your own laws – 'draft your own contracts, wills prenuptial agreements, and property deeds' and then added, 'You will need to learn the real law they don't teach in public schools.'

This is all strongly libertarian and self-reliant. But the key point was that he was thinking of ways to take practical action.

His tenth bit of advice made me laugh:

> 10. Vote for and against politicians, but don't be fooled – of all these ten ways to make a political difference, voting in a political election makes the least difference.

Of particular relevance was his fifth recommendation:

> 5. Make your own law: use strong security to protect the people, relationships, property, and data you value. Learn to defend yourself and your loved ones with weaponry. Write and use cryptography, smart

contracts, bit gold, digital cash, and other security protocols made possible by computer science.

I think it's fair to say that the dominoes were all lining up.

By early 2008, his political feeling was intensifying. He wrote, 'This blog has never before expressed an opinion about a specific political election. Unenumerated takes a long view and electioneering is generally not the most effective means of political action. Occasionally, however, there is a remarkable exception.' That exception was the outspoken libertarian Ron Paul, whose presidential candidacy Szabo fervently endorsed.

Another post later that year compared Ben Bernanke, then head of the Federal Reserve Bank, to John Law, the speculator put in charge of the French central bank in the early 1800s who presided over the Mississippi Bubble. 'John Law and the Mississippi Bubble are fairly well-known to economic historians,' Szabo said. 'But one wonders whether the supposed economic experts who run the U.S. Federal Reserve remember it.'[164] Szabo did not like the fact that Bernanke was using high-risk debt as reserves.

What is interesting is that these 'angry' posts came in 2008 – at the same time Bitcoin was being coded. Frustration was building in many people, particularly in relation to inflation. It seems Bitcoin was a practical response to it all.

But he seems to have mellowed again. When I emailed Szabo to ask if he might answer some questions by email, he said: 'Sure, as long as they're non-political.'

I asked him what his motivation was in designing bit gold to gain some insight into why he designed Bitcoin (assuming he did). 'To become a reserve, high-powered currency,' he said, 'that could be a reserve for issuing more network-efficient currencies – like gold but better.'

## How Satoshi credited everyone except himself

Satoshi was extremely careful to make sure that the likes of Adam Back and Wei Dai were properly referenced in his white paper. This much is clear from his emails prior to Bitcoin's release.

Why then did he omit any reference to Bitcoin's closest precursor, bit gold? There was no mention of it or Szabo in the Bitcoin white paper.

One interpretation of this is that Satoshi was not aware of Szabo. It was only after Adam Back's prompt that Satoshi mentioned Wei Dai. Back never prompted Satoshi about Szabo. Back tells me: 'I was probably aware of bit gold, but I wasn't on the mailing list that it was announced on, so I was more familiar with b-money.'

But it's also easy to interpret Satoshi's non-mention of Szabo as someone deliberately ignoring himself so as not to draw attention.

When Finney first replied to Satoshi in November 2008, before the first coins had even been mined, he mentioned that Bitcoin might be an implementation of Szabo's concept.[165] Satoshi replied to just about every point Finney had made, but ignored the mention of Szabo.

Only in 2010 when the Wikipedia page was being discussed did Satoshi acknowledge him, saying Bitcoin was an implementation of Szabo's bit gold idea.[166]

My interpretation is that he wanted to distance himself from the project.

It's also worth noting that when Satoshi first approached Back and Dai in August 2008, a few days prior to the release of the Bitcoin white paper, the product was just called 'ecash'. Obviously he couldn't call it that after David Chaum's experience in the 1990s. The name Bitcoin appears to have been added at the last minute – perhaps because he couldn't think of anything better, and he couldn't very well call it 'bit gold'.

In 2011 – suspiciously having ignored it till then, given what an advocate of digital cash he was – Szabo wrote a blog in defence of Bitcoin, after another blogger, Gwern, had described it as a perfect example of 'worse is better'.[167] Would Satoshi have bothered to do this? Perhaps as a red herring, yes. But anonymity is a delicate art. Silence is usually best. Red herrings are often what give you away. Would he have taken this risk? Unlikely, but maybe he felt the need to publicly defend his creation against the criticisms of a thinker he admired.

## The huge elephant in the room that I've ignored till now

There is an elephant in the room. And I've ignored it till now. My whole theory sinks or swims by it.

It's this: how good was Szabo's C++ code?

Until we can find proof of Szabo's ability with C++, and compare his C++ to the original Bitcoin code, we can't draw conclusions. My theory would be dismissed in an instant if we could only see some examples of Szabo's C++. But neither I, nor anyone I have asked, have been able to find any examples.

My anonymous veteran coder emailed me and said, 'I've

found code by Szabo in several languages, which looked similar to Satoshi's, but because they weren't in C++ specifically I remain perplexed as to whether Szabo's C++ smells like Satoshi's. Frustrating as hell!'

Wei Dai says Szabo is not known as a C++ coder,[168] but, in fact, it seems that once upon a time he might have been. There is an old resume in which he advertises his skills. And while others dismiss C++, Szabo defended it to me, 'C++ is a great language for implementing cryptographic primitives because of its efficiency.'

All in all, we're left with a flood of circumstantial evidence but no proof that Satoshi is Szabo.

It would help if denials from Szabo that he is Satoshi had been a bit more forceful. Journalist Adrian Chen asked him in 2011, 'Got any ideas/guesses as to who Satoshi is?' Szabo replied: 'I'm not going to contribute any further on this as I think he has made a great contribution and so I want to respect his desire for privacy.'[169] Szabo says he has denied it to other journalists, but actual denials are hard to find.

In my own correspondence with him, he was very helpful – but ignored every one of my questions about Satoshi and whether he had mined coins.

Wei Dai and Nick Szabo came up with b-money and bit gold independently of each other. Adam Back tells me others came up with similar ideas to his own Hashcash. Perhaps something similar happened with Bitcoin. Perhaps Satoshi's philosophical and technical roots have nothing to do with Cypherpunks. Perhaps they lie somewhere else altogether, somewhere that nobody has yet considered.

It's possible.

But I doubt it.

I think Nicholas Julius Szabo is Satoshi Nakamoto.

Heck, their initials mirror – NS/SN. Was that another little Easter egg Satoshi left us?

# Postscript

Since completing this manuscript, but before publication, I exchanged emails again with Nick Szabo – I felt it was right to alert him to the conclusions I'd drawn. I also sent him a copy of the book. He replied, 'Thanks for letting me know. I'm afraid you got it wrong doxing me as Satoshi, but I'm used to it'.

In June, Szabo began using Twitter, where he also denied being Satoshi, saying on June 6th, 2014, when it was suggested, 'Not Satoshi, but thank you.'

Szabo is well worth following on Twitter. I spent a fantastic morning looking through all the tweets he had made, retweeted or favourited. He's as interesting and polymathic as ever.

He tweets about law, smart contracts, maths (especially algebra), computer science, history, anthropology, politics and liberty, privacy, economics and finance. He seems to have a fondness for maps and to be especially interested in diet (in particular, its relationship with genes). He mentions Ethereum a great deal, but the subject he keeps coming back to is Bitcoin. His pinned tweet links to the 'best computer science paper on Bitcoin'. He comments that, 'scams are fuelled by misplaced trust. Trust math, (next best) traditional auditing. Make bad security fail early'. And he asserts that 'Trusted third party: security hole (mtGox) or large traditional bureaucracy (bank). Choose your poison.'

The first people he followed – Gavin Andreson, Andrew Miller and Peter Todd – were all heavily involved in Bitcoin from an early stage. The first companies he followed were Blockstream Project – which is 'digitizing the entire planet's assets for the betterment of all its occupants' – Ethereum and Computer Science, which gives you daily tweets about computer science.

Of note was one his retweets – Russian chess grandmaster Garry Kasparov, who said: 'Sorry, but I'm from a place where everything was "shared equally" and it wasn't as nice as some of you seem to think it would be'. It's libertarian stuff.

Despite his denial, my conclusions (or my biases) remain unchanged.

# 7

# WHY BITCOIN IS THE ENEMY OF THE STATE

*Congressman, as I have said to you before, the problem you are alluding to is the conversion of a commodity standard to fiat money...it is inevitable that the authority, which is the producer of the money supply, will have inordinate power.*
— Alan Greenspan, former Chairman of the Federal Reserve Bank

(N.B. If you have read *Life After the State*, you will already be familiar with the argument of this chapter.)

Once upon a time, gold was money.

On a gold standard, governments and banks could, broadly speaking, only print as many notes as they had the gold supply to back them. This placed a restriction on government, the same restriction we all have: we can only spend as much money as we have, or as people will lend us. (It is a little more complicated than that, but the broad point remains.)

In 1914, shortly after the beginning of the First World War, the British, French and German governments all took their countries off the gold standard. They then printed the money they needed to pay for the war. What resulted was, as we all know, one of the most terrible wars in history. Four years of unrelenting horror. Some 37 million people died. A further 50–100 million lives were lost to the Spanish flu that followed (which probably had its origins on the Western Front).[170]

If those governments could only have spent as much gold as they had in their vaults, the war would have had to end when the gold ran out. As they did not have enough gold to pay for the war to go on for long, the war really might have been over by Christmas.

But by manipulating the money system and coming off the gold standard, they enabled themselves to both print money and run up deficits (spend more money than they earn). Thus it became possible for the war to continue in the terrible way that it did.

This was the beginning of the 'fiat money' era – fiat, meaning money by command. You must accept this money as payment for goods and services, and pay taxes in it.

As this money is not backed by anything tangible, there is (almost) no limit to how much can be created. This makes inflation of some kind almost inevitable. It also gives disproportionate power to the body that is able to create the money, particularly if no significant effort is needed to create it. As Alan Greenspan said, standing before Congress, 'it is inevitable that the authority, which is the producer of the money supply, will have inordinate power'.[171]

Without their control of money, none of the wars of the

twentieth century could have dragged on to the same extent. No war has ever been fought on a transparent cash basis.

'Without the money-counterfeiting tool of government,' wrote American economist E. C. Riegel in 1949, 'there could be no war except by popular mandate, because the price would have to be consciously and immediately paid. The would-be war-maker first of all conquers and subdues his own people by the narcotic of counterfeit money. If the people would hold the veto power of war, they must deny to their government the power to counterfeit money.'[172]

Take away this power to create money and run deficits and suddenly the scope of a war is limited to the amount of money the government has. Independent money limits wars.

To me, that is the most compelling argument there is in favour of independent money. It is a force for peace.

I'm not saying there would be no wars – there were plenty of wars under a gold standard – usually entailing the abuse of that standard. But if money were beyond the control of government, wars could not be of the same magnitude as those that blighted the 20th century.

But independent money doesn't just limit wars. It limits everything a government does.

## The growth of the state

At present we live in a world where the state looks after our birth, our education, our health, often our employment, our old age and even our burial.

'Twas not ever thus.

In the UK the move towards the large state model began in the late 19th century. First, there was compulsory education. Then the Liberal Reforms of 1906–14 saw the introduction of state pensions, National Insurance and income tax. These were only small steps. It was with WWI and the abandonment of the gold standard that the role of the state in the life of an Englishman really began to grow.

America was on its own path to large government. In 1913 income tax was introduced and the Federal Reserve Bank was created to manage the dollar. In 1932, to generate the funds he wanted for his New Deal, Roosevelt confiscated Americans' gold, gave Americans dollars in exchange and then devalued the dollar. In the 1960s, under the presidency of Lyndon Johnson, the American state grew even further. Johnson's War on Poverty saw the Social Security Act, the Food Stamp Act, the Economic Opportunity Act and the Elementary and Secondary Education Act signed into law.

But these reforms, together with America's involvement in the Vietnam War, cost money. The US began printing dollars – many more dollars than its gold supply could back. This would lead to a run on America's gold by other nations, and in 1971 the US abandoned the gold standard for good and joined the rest of the world under a fiat money system.

There are many, particularly on the political left, who think the large state model the right one. There are others, particularly in the libertarian area of the political spectrum, who don't. Wherever you stand, the large state model is only possible – if not inevitable – when government controls money. If money becomes independent, then a government struggles to fund itself.

# A word about the great obfuscation that is inflation - and how it causes the wealth gap

Inflation once meant 'an increase in the supply of money and credit leading to higher prices'. Deflation meant the opposite – 'a decrease in the supply of money and credit leading to lower prices'. These meanings have, however, been distorted over time, so that inflation is now 'rising prices' and deflation 'falling prices'. It may not seem important – meanings of words change all the time – but it is.

The official method of measuring inflation, the Consumer Price Index (CPI), tracks the prices of things we commonly use – food, clothing, transport, energy and so on. From 1989 to now CPI has averaged just under 3% in both the UK and the US. But the amount of money circulating has grown at an average rate of 11.5% per year over the same period.

Money supply has also grown faster than the economy. In 1971 in the UK, there was £31 billion in circulation. Now there are just under £2,100 billion (£2.1 trillion). That is a 67-fold increase. Are we 67 times richer? A few people are. But most of us aren't. Similarly, the US has seen $800 billion become $16 trillion – a 20-fold increase.

Research by think tank Positive Money shows that only about 10% of newly created money goes into the kind of consumer goods tracked by CPI. So all CPI does is measure the effects of about 10% of money creation. What's more, many of the goods tracked by CPI face the deflationary pressures of competition and improved productivity. For example, computers and other mass-processed goods tend to fall in price.

Positive Money's research also demonstrates that 13% of

newly created money has gone into real businesses that create jobs and boost economic growth; 37% into financial markets and 40% into residential and commercial property. Is it any wonder the financial and real estate sectors have grown so disproportionately large? That's where the money's gone.

The trusted tool to deal with inflation is to raise interest rates. The effect of higher rates is that money costs more to borrow and people borrow less. So, the cost of assets that people use borrowed money to buy – houses and financial assets, especially – tends to fall.

But the last thing a government wants on its watch, particularly if an election is looming, is falling house prices or a falling stock market. Where possible, it will not want to raise rates. So how handy it is to have an official measure that 'proves' that inflation is low – especially one that ignores 77% of new money supply.

But the manipulation of money has unseen consequences. It actually causes the wealth gap.

Government printing of money, even with quantitative easing, is not quite as willy-nilly as some would have you believe. Banks actually create more money than governments. 'The majority of money in the modern economy is created by commercial banks making loans,' says the Bank of England.[173] About 96% of the money in fact – in both the US and the UK.

Electronic banking, which began in the 1980s and replaced the cash- and cheque-based economy, has made it possible for banks to do this – facilitated by the decision to ignore money-supply growth in measures of inflation.

The social consequence of this has been for the financial sector to grow disproportionately large and influential – for banks to have become 'too big to fail'. More and more people have been drawn to this sector where they can get some kind of exposure to new money creation. But elsewhere, perfectly innocent people lose out because of it. This is from *Life After the State*:

> Imagine a tiny economy. There are 20 people in it. Of these, ten each have $1 in cash, so there is $10 in the entire economy. The other ten people each have a house – these are the only assets in the economy and are each priced at $1. People quite happily buy and sell these houses for $1 each. If more houses appear in this economy, but the amount of money stays finite, the cost of houses will fall. But let us assume for now no new houses enter the economy.
>
> One person – Mr King – is suddenly able to magically create another $10 from nowhere. He decides to go out and spend some of this new money. He buys a house for $1, which the vendor is happy to sell because, based on the knowledge the vendor has, that is the fair market price. Except that it isn't because there is no longer $10 in the economy, but $20. At $1 the vendor has sold his house too cheap – and he has received devalued money in exchange.
>
> Mr King then decides to outbid the others and offers $1.50 for another house. This vendor is delighted, sells, probably feeling rather clever, and makes off with $1.50, but even he has sold his house

too cheap. Mr King, meanwhile, is developing a nice little property empire. The other vendors hear houses are now trading for $1.50 and now expect that price, which Mr King is happy to pay. In other words, house prices are gradually rising to reflect the new money in circulation.

There are some big losers in this process – the people who each had $1. The purchasing power of their money is now no longer enough to buy the house they were previously able to buy. Ultimately, their purchasing power will halve because there is twice as much money in circulation. They haven't acted imprudently in any way – they haven't even acted – yet they are made poorer by this process of other people creating new money.

What about the people owning houses? How have they done? Eventually, houses prices in this economy will rise to $2 – there are ten houses and $20 in circulation. The price of their houses should rise to reflect this extra money in circulation, so – as long as they didn't sell – they come out even. They might think they are richer because their house now costs $20, but this is a delusion: it is the same house. They have just survived the inflation, nothing more. If, however, they were one of the early vendors who sold for $1 or $1.50, now they cannot afford to buy back the house they previously sold. They are 'priced out' and poorer.

Meanwhile, Mr King has done extremely well. He benefits, of course, as the recipient of a load of newly created money. But he was also able to buy houses for $1 and $1.50, before they rose in price to reflect the new money in circulation, so, with his houses now valued at $2, he profits from the asset-price inflation too. Wealth, which was originally spread evenly through our tiny economy, has insidiously transferred from cash-holders and those who sold their houses early to Mr King.

As a consequence of this process not only has wealth transferred, but those operating in our tiny economy no longer focus on making things. Instead they look for signs of future money creation and speculate on those signs, because there is more money to be made that way.[174]

The process is continuous and relentless. Economists call it the Cantillon effect, after the 18th-century French-Irish economist, Richard Cantillon.

If you own the assets or if you operate in the sectors that benefit from all this newly created money – the financial sector and, in the case of the UK, the London property in which it mostly lives – you make spectacular gains. But if you don't own these assets – and most young people don't – you get left behind, and the wealth gap gets bigger.

We are constantly told that hard work pays. If you start out with nothing, the way to better your lot is to work hard. But significantly bettering your lot is not so easy these days because wages have not kept up with the increase in the money supply.

In the US wages have gone from around $6,000 per annum in 1971 to $44,000 today.[175] So, while the money supply in the US has increased by 2,000%, wages have increased by 750%. The inequality in the UK is greater. Money supply has increased by 6,700%, wages by just 1,250%.[176] Wages, in short, have failed to keep up with inflation.

In addition, you are also taxed heavily on your wages – and the harder you work, the more you are taxed.

At the same time, many of the assets you might want to buy are rising in price and getting further out of reach. Those that own the assets you want to buy are not taxed on their gains, unless they actually sell – and capital gains tax is lower than income tax.

The result is a system in which labour is penalized, and capital and assets are not. Inflation and income tax between them actually increase the wealth gap.

Many families now find themselves having to work longer hours, with both spouses in the workplace, taking on larger debts and having fewer children just to maintain an ordinary middle-class lifestyle. Many of their children face unprecedented levels of debt and, in many places, will never be able to buy a house.

What is happening is an insidious transfer of wealth from those that don't own the right assets or operate in the right sectors to those that do. This process will not stop until inflation is measured accurately and honestly and until taxation is reformed.

Forget property – *money* is theft.

# Why Bitcoin is libertarian Utopia

There are four ways a government funds its activities.

The first is through taxation – income tax, property tax, road tax, sales tax, corporation tax, import duties and so on. Income tax is by far the largest earner – about 40% of government revenue in the US and 30% in the UK (50% if you include National Insurance). It is easy to collect because it is levied at source. Add to taxation various rents and income from its activities and the sale of assets.

The second way a government funds itself is through debt. Government borrows money through the bond markets.

The third is by actually creating money – printing it and creating it by other means such as quantitative easing.

The fourth is by manipulating money – inflation. We have just seen how insidious this is.

Let's be idealistic for a moment and imagine that Bitcoin and other independent monies become the globally preferred means to make and receive payment. I do not see this as at all likely in the short term. But in the longer term, I do – and the implications are enormous.

In a flash, the ability for a government to fund itself through the manipulation of money disappears. You can't obfuscate bitcoin supply – inflation is transparent. You can't 'quantitatively ease' bitcoins. Governments – without a very aggressive and potentially impractical bitcoin confiscation scheme – will struggle to use your bitcoins to bail themselves out. Deficit spending becomes impossible – you can't spend bitcoins you don't have. Central and private banks can't create bitcoins when it suits them, and governments can't print bitcoins (they'd have to compete to mine coins along with everyone else).

It all means you don't have to pay the price for the mistakes of governments and banks. They do. They will have to act more prudently or go under.

If it can't fund itself though the manipulation or printing of money, a government would have to rely more on borrowing. But even that option is not as appealing as it once was. A government can no longer devalue its debt through inflation or the suppression of interest rates. With no control over money, government borrowing rates would have to increase to cover for the very real risk of default.

So, government will find itself forced to live off its tax revenue. But, again, Bitcoin could also change the way we are taxed.

If workers are paid in bitcoins, income tax will become much harder to levy at source. Many people will do what corporations and the self-employed already do – try to find legitimate ways – and in some cases illegitimate ways – to reduce the amount of tax they have to pay. And if governments demand too much tax, people look for ways to avoid it – it will be no different with Bitcoin. It will mean greater state resources are required to stop evaders and avoiders. An investigation might not be worth the cost for the amount it levies. This, of course, raises all sorts of moral issues.

But taxation, in its current form, will be harder to enforce and more costly to levy. In all probability, we'll move towards the taxation of consumption and assets, rather than labour – a land value tax, even (see the footnote for more on land value tax[177]).

Charles Hoskinson, CEO of Ethereum – dubbed 'Bitcoin 2.0' – says to me:

> I think it's going to go to a national sales tax. If you're a business you're going to probably have a physical footprint because you have warehouses, you have to store products, you have a store front, you have to register with the government. If you're an Internet business, maybe then you can live 100% in the cloud. But let's say for the sake of the argument you have to have a physical presence, then it's easy for the government to levy upon business standards like sales tax.
>
> While it's going to become increasingly more difficult to know how much money people are making, it's still going to be relatively easy for governments to collect sales tax on businesses and keep businesses in compliance because businesses are not in the habit of evading income tax or evading sales taxes. So I think we're probably going to see a larger transition towards a national sales tax and a reduction, either in legislation or in feasibility, of income tax.

Why is Bitcoin libertarian Utopia? Libertarians tend be of the view that most government action, even if well intended, has negative consequences. Losing control of money means that, suddenly, governments are more limited in what they can do. There might be fewer wars, there might also be less state welfare. That's a frightening thought for many, but the libertarian view is that welfare would be both cheaper, more effective and more widespread if the state stayed out of it.

But it's not just that Bitcoin limits government. It also has the potential to redistribute wealth. A deflationary system of money means savers are rewarded rather than debtors – a paradigm shift in the way things work. A society that transparently taxes consumption rather than production means labour is rewarded rather than penalized. A money that is free of banks means people can bypass banking systems. The huge concentrations of money and power that have found their way into the financial sector can finally be diluted. There is no insidious transfer of wealth to 'Mr King'.

Suddenly the enormous cost of the state – and your government is the most expensive purchase you will ever make – is lightened. Being taxed less and compensated for their labour in a currency with increasing purchasing power means workers really do have a chance to better their lot.

As Satoshi said, Bitcoin is 'very attractive to the libertarian viewpoint if we can explain it properly'.[178] Ain't it so.

# 8

# HOW BITCOIN WILL CHANGE THE WORLD

*Bitcoin is the beginning of something great: a currency without a government, something necessary and imperative.*

— Nassim Taleb, author and statistician

My stepfather's parents, who were Jewish, fled Germany in 1936. Luckily for them, they had gold – and they used some of it to bribe their way out. That same gold had protected them during the madness of the Weimar hyperinflation 14 years earlier.

Wanting to get as far as possible from the dangers they perceived in Europe, they went to South Africa. The last of the gold they had managed to smuggle out of Germany helped them to get started in their new life there.

They had two children. Some years later, one of them, my stepfather, would also find himself wanting to 'get out'. He decided he didn't like what was happening in South Africa and in the 1970s became determined to leave. However, there were capital controls in those days. He could go, but he couldn't take his money with him.

The way he got round the problem, like his parents before him, was with gold. He bought 60 Krugerrands (about $80,000 in today's money) and got on a flight to London. Those 60 Krugers were enough to get him started in his new life in the UK.

But he had to take considerable risk. He could have lost those Krugers, or they might have been stolen or confiscated. There was also the possibility he would be caught and charged with smuggling.

In the 1970s there were capital controls across the West. Until 1979 in the UK you had to get permission to take more than £25 – less than 50 dollars – abroad.[179] Those controls may not exist to anything like the same extent now, but they do exist elsewhere.

China, for example, is the world's second-largest economy, yet individuals may not withdraw more than $50,000 per annum from the country.

The banking crisis in Cyprus in 2013 saw capital controls introduced there. Currently, cash withdrawals are limited to €300 a day, the cashing of cheques is banned and large cash transfers are vetted. Accounts with over €100,000 saw funds confiscated. Capital controls now seem to be being imposed in the Ukraine due to its current instability.

Reports suggest nationals are finding it harder and harder to get their money out of Spain and other parts of impoverished Southern Europe, and the insolvency of Spain's banks makes another banking crisis in the region look probable. The investment bank JP Morgan has declared it is 'inevitable that capital controls and a capital freeze will be imposed'[180] in Southern Europe; senior employees tell me many of their current strategies are based on this inevitability.

Where there is an economic or political crisis, capital controls often follow. Innocent people are made to pay for the profligacies of their banks, their financial system or their governments.

Bitcoin has been dubbed 'money without government' and 'money without borders'. You can send money to another country as easily as you can an email, and nearly as instantly. There is no need to smuggle 60 Krugerrands in your pocket if you're fleeing an oppressive regime.

People are already starting to use Bitcoin in this way. When the Cypriot banking crisis hit during the spring of 2013 and fear of capital controls loomed across Southern Europe, the bitcoin price rose from about $15 to north of $200. In the latter part of 2013, the price ballooned again, rising from about $130 to over $1,000 due to Chinese interest. Much of that interest was speculative, but some of it was also money fleeing the country. Shanghai resident Zennon Kapron declared, 'some people have the equivalent of tens of millions in dollar-equivalent value in China and they want to get it out. They want to send their children to school in Canada, the US, Australia. Wealthy families, new and old money — it's not a lack of trust in the local system, it's just a need to diversify their investments.'[181]

With Bitcoin, suddenly capital controls do not apply as they once did. This frees up the possibilities for money laundering and other illicit activity, of course, but it also frees up people. The implications of this possibility to instantly transfer wealth or ownership across borders without interference are, I think, considerable.

It means borders would lose much of their significance.

## Why Bitcoin is an irresistible force

These kinds of stories are compelling to those that distrust governments, but they will not be enough to take Bitcoin into mainstream use.

What will take Bitcoin – or some other currency that replicates and improves the technology – into the mainstream is the efficiency and simplicity of its payment system and the savings it makes for its users. The political implications of Bitcoin are appealing to some, but it is the technology that will make it irresistible to the wider world. I'll explain.

I earn my living as a writer, a speaker and a comedian. I'm based in the UK. With the growth of the internet and all accompanying media, I find I am hired for more and more work overseas – and for much of it, I don't need to leave my desk.

As a writer, I might be asked to write articles for publications overseas. Over the last year, for example, I've been asked to write for publications in the US, Canada, Germany, Singapore and Australia.

With my irresistibly charming English accent, I am often asked to voice all sorts of different media overseas. It might be a documentary for Discovery or National Geographic in the US, it might be a video game made somewhere in Asia, a video for a Canadian mining company or some new altcoin based in the ether.

I am often asked to speak or do gigs overseas. In the last

year or two I've done gigs or spoken in South Africa, Canada, the US, Dubai, Germany, Ireland and Romania.

International payment is almost always a headache. IBAN numbers, SWIFT codes, BIC codes, foreign exchange charges, fees to send money, fees to receive money, money getting lost, different time zones and bank opening hours and the time it takes for money to actually transfer. All in all, payment is needlessly expensive and inefficient. It's verging on the archaic.

For one-off payments of more than $1,000, the $50 or $100 in costs are bearable, though they still gall – and if you do regular work for somebody, those costs compound, as does the gall factor. But for a small job of $50, $100 or $200, the costs of transferring money are such that jobs are not worth doing. Which means the exchange is less likely to take place.

Some use PayPal to get around the problem, and PayPal can work well. But it is not cheap. PayPal also has a habit of freezing accounts; and many people, for various reasons, do not have accounts. You need a credit card to open a PayPal account, but not everybody can get a credit card. Even in the US, almost 30% of the population does not have a credit card.[182] In the developing world, the percentage is much higher. In India, for example, 79% of the 1.2 billion people who live there don't have cards.[183] Most of them will have smart phones first.

'Existing payment systems are often quite expensive', says University of Chicago Professor of Law Eric Posner, 'either because somebody effectively has a monopoly, there are a lot of government regulations that are costly to comply with, or the companies that offer these services provide certain protections that people want and are willing to pay for. In the case of Bitcoin as it stands now, these costs are largely avoided, at least to the extent that you can technically send bitcoins from one wallet to another wallet without incurring fees; no middlemen are required to do this.'[184]

Of course, there are costs involved with using Bitcoin. If you convert bitcoins to your local national currency, there are fees. If you use a Bitcoin service provider (a Bitcoin bank, basically) such as Coinbase or Bitpay, there will be fees there too. There is the risk of having your bitcoins stolen, which is another cost in itself. But these costs can all be avoided, if so desired. And the more people that are buying and selling things with bitcoins, the less need there is to actually leave the network – and take on the expense of doing so.

Warren Buffett, the legendary billionaire, dismisses the idea that a bitcoin has any value. 'It's a mirage,' he says. 'Stay away. The idea that it has some huge intrinsic value is just a joke.'[185] But even he – a notorious techno-sceptic – sees the potential of the technology. 'It's a very effective way of trans-mitting money,'[186] he says.

The Bitcoin protocol offers enormous savings for people who wish to do business with each other using it – particu-larly at the smaller end of the business scale. These savings and efficiencies mean that many exchanges that would not be possible under existing payments systems can now happen. It is by exchange that people prosper and progress. I asked Nick Szabo if Bitcoin can change the world. 'Yes it can,' he said. 'By lowering transaction costs for a wide variety of people that are shut out of the current financial system.'

Goldman Sachs IT analyst Roman Leal has made some rough calculations as to the savings that Bitcoin could have made possible globally in electronic payment in 2013. There's no proving the block chain could yet manage such levels of volume, and Leal makes the point that regulatory and operating costs for Bitcoin could quite easily rise, while the competition it brings to existing payment services means these costs will probably fall. Even so, the numbers are startling.

Let's start with a simple money transfer. Consumers end up paying as much as 10% of the total amount transferred if they use a money transfer network such as Western Union. This fee covers agents' commissions, forex and access to the network. With Bitcoin that fee could of course be zero – or 1% if you use a Bitcoin service provider such as Bitpay or Coinbase. There were $49 billion of transaction fees globally in 2013 on about $550 billion of remittances. With Bitcoin those fees fall by 90% to just $5.5 billion.[187] That would mean an extra $43 billion of money actually makes it into people's pockets.

Looking next at electronic payments in retail, currently retailers pay from about 2.5% to 3% in transaction fees. In 2013, global transaction fees at retail point of sale were $260 billion on over $10 trillion of sales. Had Bitcoin been used (again using a 1% estimated fee) the number would be $104 billion – a saving of almost $150 billion.[188] Leal notes that all 'merchants would realize sizable savings' by using Bitcoin, but small merchants will benefit most. They 'can reduce their payment processing fees by at least half'.[189] That is a compelling number for a business that runs on low margins.

As long as Bitcoin keeps its costs down, these kinds of savings will become irresistible.

# Empowering the great unbanked

In the midst of the boom that China has enjoyed over the last 25 years, something quite extraordinary happened.

When it developed its telecommunications infrastructure, it hardly laid down any cables and wires. Technology was at such a point where China was able to bypass all that and go straight to wireless.

It's very easy to get all excited and imagine something similar with developing Third World nations by-passing banks and banking infrastructure altogether and going straight to Bitcoin. In fact, something similar is already happening – but it doesn't involve Bitcoin. It is most apparent in Kenya with the M-Pesa. M stands for mobile. Pesa is Swahili for money – so you have 'mobile money'.

It began quite organically in the early 2000s in various parts of Africa. People started transferring their mobile phone minutes – their airtime credits – to friends or family. This airtime, of course, has a definite value. Based on a 'real thing' it would become a modern day commodity currency. Safaricom and Vodafone both picked up on the practice and brought in systems to both regulate and facilitate it. You can send airtime, M-Pesas, by text (SMS) message.

As early as 2009, such was the pace at which the M-Pesa was expanding, Kenyan banks actually lobbied the government to audit M-Pesa in an attempt to slow its growth. But it made little difference. Now something like two-thirds of Kenyans now use the M-Pesa and as much as 43% of national GDP flows through it.[190]

Only 40% of Kenyans have a bank account.[191] According to the World Bank, in 2012 over 70% had a mobile phone.[192]

With the M-Pesa, the 'unbanked' now have access to basic financial services. People can deposit and withdraw money, transfer money (even to non-users), pay bills, buy airtime and, in some cases, actually transfer money to a bank account. They can even obtain credit. This is precisely how Szabo envisages Bitcoin changing the world. Mobile phones are replacing banks.

'Financial inclusion is reported to be at 80% in Kenya', says Sitoyo Lopokoiyit of Safaricom. 'When you remove mobile money, it drops to 23%. So you can see what mobile money does for financial inclusion in Kenya.'[193]

The M-Pesa has been launched in Tanzania, South Africa, India, Afghanistan and Eastern Europe. It has had some success in Afghanistan and Tanzania, rather less in South Africa – but nowhere has it worked as well as in Kenya.

Steps are currently being taken to launch it in India. I've spoken to some of the venture capitalists involved. They are extremely bullish about the short-term prospects – much more so than they are of Bitcoin's, for two simple reasons.

The first is internet connectivity. Most of rural Asia and rural Africa (not to mention rural England) does not yet have extensive internet coverage. It's coming, but it's still several years away. Until they do, the possibilities of Bitcoin are extremely limited for day-to-day use.

These regions do, however, have mobile phone coverage. Smart phones may still be prohibitively expensive, but mobile phones are not. More and more people own one and a mobile is enough to transact via M-Pesa.

Second is M-Pesa's ease of use. Older, technologically naïve, rural folk will find it easier to get to grips with SMS payments than they will with downloading Bitcoin wallets and all the rest of it.

The M-Pesa is a centralized money issued by mobile phone networks, unlike the decentralized open source creation that is Bitcoin. The M-Pesa has more limited use and less potential functionality than Bitcoin. It is not a money without borders. But given the stage of development that much of rural Asia and Africa is at, I'm inclined to agree that the M-Pesa has greater potential in these parts of the world over the next few years. It also has significant first-mover advantage.

But the prospects of the M-Pesa emphasize the point that people the world over need better systems of sending money and that these better systems are coming.

There are some 640,000 villages in India. Seventy-two per cent of India's 1.2 billion people live in them. The other 28% live in towns or cities.[194] Over half of India's population don't have bank accounts[195] – and the rural population is considerably more than 50% 'unbanked'. In 2000 the Indian government launched a campaign to get people banking, but now 90% of the 100 million accounts that were opened are dormant.[196]

It's typical for men to leave rural villages and head to larger towns or cities to find work. How do they send money home? (The rural Mexican working in the US has a similar problem.)

Even if they do have bank accounts, going to a bank to send money can involve taking time off work – which they might not want or might not be able to do. Their wife in all probability will not have a bank account. If she does, the nearest bank might be more than a day's travel away – so collecting the money is inconvenient and potentially expensive for her as well.

The post office is the way that some people send money. But, again, most villages don't have a post office. India has 155,000 post offices in total, many of them in towns and cities, for its 640,000 villages.

Western Union and other similar organizations are another possibility. But we already know about the 10% fees. Venture capitalists tell me you can add another 10% by the time you factor in the collection costs (travel and accommodation) and the working hours lost while the money is being sent.

With the M-Pesa, and, eventually, Bitcoin, they don't need to leave home.

India, and much of rural Asia, Africa and South America, badly need a simple, cheap way to transfer money. One day Bitcoin or some development of it will meet that need. SMS payment systems are already being developed for Bitcoin, but for now it looks as though the simplicity and investment capital behind the M-Pesa will win that particular battle.

But it is still a battle that is being won by a non-government currency, beyond traditional banking. And, through the M-Pesa and other currencies like it, the third world can bypass traditional banking, just as China bypassed cables and went straight to wireless.

The monopoly on money and payments that banks have held for so long is under threat from cheaper, more efficient systems.

The implications for banking as we know it are considerable.

But so are the implications for people.

# Why Bitcoin could have a greater impact than the internet

Governments, generally, keep a tight control on the movements of money throughout the world. This is not by accident. There are terrorist concerns, money-laundering concerns, tax concerns – all sorts of reasons.

Bitcoin has suddenly made it easy to move money around without people knowing about it. There is going to be a lot of friction between know-your-customer, anti-money laundering and other regulations in the traditional money movement system and this new system – especially between the developing world and the developed world.

Take the remittance business between the US and Mexico.

One of the highest contributors to Mexican GDP is actually money sent from economic migrants in the United States to family members back home. Over the last ten years this has averaged almost $25 billion – which is about 10% of Mexican GDP. (China, India and the rest of Latin America combined actually send greater amounts; though Mexicans comprise about 55% of the foreign-born US population.)

At present, 7–10% of money sent home to Mexico is consumed in the remittance process. Bitcoin, of course, has made it possible to do this at zero cost. As more and more people adopt this technology and companies offer this service, it's going to be more and more difficult for the United States to monitor and control that money exodus.

That is going to present geopolitical problems and create tension between the US and Mexico.

On the other hand, of the seven billion people in the

world, only around two billion are banked and participate in ecommerce. Yet about 5.5 billion have at least some access to the internet.

That's a potential 3.5 billion people who could participate in ecommerce, but don't because they don't have access to the necessary financial infrastructure.

With this new decentralized money-movement system, the developed world now has potentially 3.5 billion new people to outsource jobs to, to sell products to and to receive products from. That is a lot of new trade.

It's very beneficial to the economy as a whole – even if it isn't for existing systems.

Ethereum's Charles Hoskinson says to me, 'I think it's going to have probably as big of an impact on the world as the internet. The internet made communications super easy, but it showed that our money system doesn't work very well. And now we have a new money system that's started to materialize'.

This money system will grow bigger and better. It's going to improve and increase commerce. It could unleash a huge global economic boom, as good for developing nations as it is for the developed.

The Bitcoin technology has laid the foundations for a dramatic increase in exchange. And, of course, exchange is the crucial process by which mankind prospers and progresses.

# 9

# A BILLION-DOLLAR HEDGE FUND MANAGER AND A SUPER-SMART MATHEMATICIAN FORECAST THE FUTURE

*[Bitcoin] is a techno tour de force.*

— Bill Gates, computer programmer, founder of Microsoft

It was a breakthrough technology. Everyone agreed about that.

And it worked.

But as the open-source community developed it, a number of discussions, sometimes heated ones, broke out as to which direction Bitcoin should take. Some didn't like the fact that bitcoin mining consumed so much power, citing ecological reasons. Others didn't like the deflationary characteristics of the coin. Others felt there could be more usability – it should do more than just be a system of payment.

But as Bitcoin grew in value, more money was at stake. Shifts in direction could have serious financial ramifications. So, while the community discussed ideas, few changes were made.

Instead, coders began to develop alternative cryptocurrencies, aping some aspects of Bitcoin but changing others. These were known as altcoins.

There are now 300 or more kinds of altcoin. Many of them are scams and get-rich-quick schemes. Many of them are simply experiments. Most of them will amount – or already have amounted – to nothing. But some of them are quite legitimate.

At present, they comprise just a few per cent of the entire cryptocurrency market cap. At $500 a coin, the market cap of Bitcoin stands at around $6.5 billion. All the other altcoins combined amount to about $350,000.

Bitcoin has attracted all the publicity. Bitcoin has all the infrastructure and investment. For now Bitcoin dominates the space.

But the altcoins may one day come to rival Bitcoin.

Litecoin is said to be silver to Bitcoin's gold. It has faster transaction time confirmation than Bitcoin, making it a better system of payment. It also claims its storage efficiency is better.

Like Litecoin, Dogecoin also has faster transaction time confirmation. It is a more inflationary system – there is no limit to supply and it has a faster coin production schedule. Its primary use has been for online tipping and fundraising – you see something you like, you give them some dogecoins.

Some coins have been developed which are more private and anonymous. Darkcoin is currently the most famous of these. Transactions are pooled together in its block chain, so they cannot be traced back to individual wallets. No prizes for guessing where Darkcoin is going to find use.

Other coins have greater functionality. Mastercoin is used to send smart contracts and smart properties. Primecoin searches for chains of prime numbers during the mining process – so it has use in mathematical research. Namecoin acts as a decentralized domain name server outside of the Internet Corporation for Assigned Names and Numbers (ICANN), which co-ordinates the internet's global domain name system. This provides added protection during outages, but it also makes censorship that much more problematic, and decentralizes the American-centric control of the domain name system.

Ripple aims to allow instant, secure and 'nearly free' payment, exchange and remittance of any fiat currency, cryptocurrency, commodity or other unit of value from air miles to mobile minutes. It does not consume energy in the way that bitcoin mining does. It also has a transaction time confirmation of between two and five seconds.

Ethereum is combining Bitcoin's decentralized mining system with a software development platform – more on this in a moment.

It's not hard to envisage a future with hundreds of different altcoins – all with their own quirks and uses. Perhaps you will have many different wallets with many different coins – just as now, you have different currencies, air miles, rewards points and so on. Or, perhaps, just a handful will come to dominate – and maybe those coins that will dominate have not yet even been invented. There is a long way to go.

One thing is for sure: the next generation of cryptocurrencies is just beginning.

## The multimillionaire hedge fund manager who is risking it all for cryptos

This is no squat in Bow.

It is a large house in Chelsea.

There are no broken windows or aggressive notices.

The front door is immaculately painted, the brass door ware is gleaming and the garden is green and kempt.

When I ring the bell, a formally dressed housekeeper answers almost immediately.

She shows me into the drawing room, where, after a moment or two, the master of the house and his wife come to greet me. The wife is very glamorous. For an informal Sunday, there is a lot of jewellery going on. She offers me tea, passes my order on to the housekeeper, and then politely excuses herself. She knows the men are here to talk about this Bitcoin thing that her husband is suddenly so interested in.

We'll call him 'Philip'.

Mid-forties, trimmed, greying blonde hair, military bearing, strong grip, clear blue eyes that are not scared to meet yours.

He manages a multi-billion-dollar hedge fund born after the collapse of the Dotcom bubble.

'The internet bubble was ahead of its time,' he says. 'In 2000, when prices were high, the internet was already ten years old, but for most people it didn't work in their house. Most people didn't have access to email, most people didn't know what a browser was or a website or a URL. Now everyone understands all this stuff without a problem. Price bubbles are always ahead of their time.'

He laughs.

'In 1995, my boss told me email would never catch on and the world would be fine using fax machines.

'People are going to be very sceptical about crypto for a very long time. And eventually you'll wake up one day in a decade or something and they will become everyday. All the funny new terminology like 'difficulty' and 'hashrate' and 'wallet' and 'block chain', and all these new expressions no one understands will become second nature to everyone.'

This successful banker is considering walking away from what is, clearly, a very well paid job. But why?

'For me the big problem is the market,' he says. 'We live in a post-QE [quantitive easing] world and there's no value in anything. There's definitely going to be some kind of reset in my opinion. Stock markets are fully valued in the western world, certainly in America where there's been the most QE. Other markets just look like they're in trouble – Japan and so on. China has got its own difficulties with maintaining this high growth rate, which seems to be unsustainable, and other emerging markets are feeding off that. And so it's hard to see how the case for global growth is a good one. When you look at fixed income markets, yields have not been this low in living memory. So there's no return, there's low nominal GDP growth, there's no inflation. Put it all together it's pretty hard to find some good investments.

'The world is looking for something – for a new trick. I think that crypto may well be that thing.'

I ask him when he first started looking at Bitcoin?

'Early 2013. I went to a conference to find out what was going on. I bought some and played about to find out how it works. I tested a couple of exchanges, a Bitcoin ATM; I even bought a glass of wine at a bar in Chamonix. I've been fascinated ever since, but I'm still not confident in my heart of hearts as to why the world actually needs it, how it's going to work in the future. And I also don't fully trust the system, so haven't yet committed significant capital. So I sympathize with the sceptic views. But at the same time I think that all those problems are being solved one by one and I hope to contribute to that as well.

'I watched that explosive Bitcoin price move in late 2013 and it was mesmerising. You could see the excitement in all the people who owned all these altcoins. Significant wealth was created out of thin air in moments and, of course, it's all evaporated since in most cases. There are only two or three coins that have really maintained any sort of value.'

So, how is he planning to get involved?

'Looking at the crypto world, I recognized that a lot of sites were very amateur. A lot of the data was amateur, incomplete, disjointed. As a fund manager, my instinct is to tidy it all up – log all the sources of data and repackage them in a way that's more digestible and more complete. Although the good data on Bitcoin is quite good, there's really just not enough to be able to make complete decisions on whether you'd actually invest in it on an institutional basis. With your responsibilities as a fund manager, you couldn't honestly say that Bitcoin is ready for mainstream institutional investment.

'And so I'm trying to answer all the questions we all want answered. Is this thing real? Is the network real? Is it a bunch of spivs who are just having a bit of fun? Is it all about buying drugs? Or is it actually a new digital asset class, which is a natural extension of the growth of the internet?

'The first thing I want to do is accurately be able to measure the state of the market. So we needed a proper index. It's quite easy to get prices and sort of mix them together and create an index, but actually we wanted to get access to the networks of all the various different coins. We wanted to put in prices and also other inputs from social media and so on, and we want to be in a position where we can ask the questions, is this thing real? Is there a proper network with real transactions? And the way you can do that is by trying to eliminate speculative volume so you can understand what the real use actually is. And if you can find a coin that's actually got a growing network, then it's a highly valuable asset for the future.

'What we're doing here is trying to assess this as an institutional asset class. If it comes up with a green light, then I think we'll find Wall Street will be all over it in no time. Goldman Sachs and UBS have already published notes. Bloomberg publishes the Bitcoin price. Bitcoin is being taken seriously and it is being looked at. To say that Wall Street's unaware and carrying on regardless isn't true. Some people are waking up.

'Of course the vast majority of people in the financial world either think it's a scam or simply don't care. I think many would change their minds if they bothered to study it. I'm yet to meet an informed bear.

'I'm not going to make this decision lightly. One's got to be absolutely certain that this crypto space is real. And I've been asking the question for nine months and I'm pretty convinced it is real, but I don't quite know how or why. And the key is – why do we need Bitcoin and cryptos in the future? It's obviously a brilliant idea and it's not going to go away, I'm certain of that, but why do we actually need it?'

'So,' I ask him. 'What do *you* think? Do we need it?'

'I'm going to ask you a question,' he suddenly says. 'How often do you cross a border each year?'

'Twenty times, maybe?' I venture.

'Yes, I think the average person would be slightly less than that, Dominic; you are a mover and shaker. But how many times do you cross a border online each day?'

'God knows.'

'Hundreds, right?'

He continues:

'So here we are with this idea of 'on the internet they don't really have borders' and I think that's an important point. When we're talking about real transactions and you say, 'Okay, well Bitcoin, it gets rid of the banking system and so on. Great, so we go to Paris, we buy lunch and, assuming the restaurant accepts Bitcoin, we knock out some nasty thieves from Visa and MasterCard, great. I get that, but that's not going to change the world. And if necessary Visa and MasterCard will drop their prices to compete so there could be a nice pressure – and about time.

'Getting back to the basics of the argument, is Bitcoin a store of value or is it a means of exchange? And it's trying to be both because, essentially, it's a gold bar that you can email which is rather nice, because when I try to email a gold bar I struggle to get it into the socket. In that sense, cryptos really do work and very well.

'But as a store of value you really wouldn't want the

volatility that it has. The average volatility over the last five years for Bitcoin has been 110% and higher for altcoins. For gold it's 18%, for silver it's 28% and for the stock market it's about 15%. For the dollar it's about 5%. So you are dealing with something that's extraordinarily volatile and, as it matures, which, hopefully, it will, then the volatility will come down – presumably once it reaches a much higher price.

'The other way volatility could fall is by having a deeper order book. So, of course, there's a chicken and egg here because, if institutional investors become buyers, then falls won't be as severe because there's going to be more depth in the market. Certainly, there will be more sellers when the price rises, so that will reduce the volatility as the number of participants in the market increases. The whole thing's still very immature.

'The store of value argument makes sense, but I can't think that many people would see Bitcoin as a safe haven, as things stand.

'This idea about crossing borders many times a day on the internet...Well, imagine there's a blogger in Australia and they've written a nice article and actually they want to be paid a little bit of money when people read their thing. He's not set up on Visa, you don't want to type out all this stuff on a credit card. Surely, if you were to pay him 50p's worth of bitcoin for this incredible article that he's written, or a piece of data that he's calculated that for some reason has value to you, it enables little transactions like that to happen on a vast scale. You can do it quickly and simply and get rid of all this noise in the middle. Ironically, I think cryptos are more likely to push the world towards paid content than the other way around – because they enable it in a way that wasn't possible before.

'Imagine there's a situation where there's some wonderful exposé that's just happened. Let's say Victoria Beckham is caught having an affair or something like that, and it's released on a blog with a live video. For the next 15 minutes this is the most important piece of web real estate in the world. You can just imagine an advertising system that's auctioned a space above that video via a Bitcoin-based system that's automatically picked up the traffic levels. The people buy the adverts through a bit of artificial intelligence that has just gone and made the decision to spend your Bitcoin budget for the day there – as opposed to the current system, which is probably not speedy enough. And so I imagine the whole idea of artificial intelligence and computers thinking for themselves and exchanging value, without us even touching the keys. I would rather load up my computer with bitcoins to do that job than let it have access to my bank account. What I am suggesting is open source. No middlemen. Just a vast ecosystem in which to exchange value for a whole host of reasons that I can't even imagine today.'

'Is crypto actually going to replace fiat?' I ask him. 'Are we talking about a new form of money here? Or is it something else?'

'There's no reason why one day they couldn't put the dollar onto the block chain, as it were, and make it cryptographic, so that you can email it around the world as you do Bitcoin. They probably should do that, but it's still going to be centralized. Cash pays interest, it's controlled by the state, it has an exchange rate and an assumed rate of inflation. Cash is cash. Commodities are commodities. Cryptos are somewhere in the middle. They've got commodity-like characteristics and they've got transactional capability as well. It's a new asset class.'

'What's a better buy?' I ask him. 'A hundred grand's worth of gold at $1,300 an ounce or a hundred grand's worth of bitcoins at $500?'

Without pausing, he answers.

'If you want to make lots of money, crypto; if you want to preserve your wealth, gold.

'The world needs bubbles. I think they're an inevitability of the current system and we're always looking for a good candidate, but it's got to be credible. We're not just going to go and inflate tulips in this day and age.'

'How would you invest in Bitcoin?' I ask him.

'Well, I think that what is more interesting is to find a good altcoin – to find a real network that's growing that's not Bitcoin. I think Bitcoin itself is a very interesting investment. You should probably have some money there. But on the side if you want to make the real money, the catch-up trade – some altcoins. I think your first trade should just be $50 to try and learn how the system works. Don't do anything until you're absolutely comfortable with how the system works. Then I suggest you go and put 90% of your crypto book into bitcoins and 10% into altcoins. To find the good ones, don't believe the stories and avoid hype. Avoid new coins, they are actually worthless most of the time, and they've got no network. Stick to the ones that have been around for a while.

'As for companies, I don't think there's a single investment that you can make that's non-private at this moment. You can buy a hedge fund that owns bitcoins, but you may as well do it yourself.

'Most people have got more money in their pension fund, their 401k plans or their ISAs, so if you can have a vehicle to own a wacky asset, that enables crypto investment using these pools, then that's an incredibly attractive proposition. Like the gold ETFs. They solved a legal problem. The first person to package Bitcoin for the mass market will make a fortune.

'That is what we're hoping to do.'

# How Bitcoin is just the start of something much, much bigger

Ethereum is probably the most talked-about development in cryptography at present. Some call it Bitcoin 2.0.

It combines the decentralized mining system central to Bitcoin with a software development platform. Its founders say the potential applications are unlimited: from peer-to-peer betting, to financial derivatives, to identity and reputation systems, to insurance and legal contracts.

Some say Satoshi Nakamoto may now even be working for Ethereum.

Its former CEO is Charles Hoskinson. A bespectacled, bearded, extremely bright, friendly and fast-talking mathematician.

I met him over Skype.

I wanted to talk to him about Ethereum. But there was something else. I'd been tipped off that he was holding copies of all the private emails Satoshi had sent when Bitcoin was being developed. People had handed copies of their correspondence with Satoshi over to him, on the understanding that Hoskinson would archive it all and make it publically viewable. But, once he had collated all the emails, something changed his mind. He now wouldn't let anyone, including me, see them without Satoshi's express permission.

'That's not something I'm ever going to get,' he says laughing.

I asked him about his background.

'I started as a mathematician in analytic number theory, and then I moved into cryptography because the problems were a fair bit more applied and interesting. And I worked for a variety of government and private interests.

'Imagine doing a Google search, but not having Google know what you're searching for. Or maybe navigating with Google Maps on your cell phone, but not having Google know where you're going. Basically, operating on encrypted data without ever decrypting it. That's what my most recent cryptographic projects before going into Bitcoin were about. It's called fully homomorphic encryption – really good awesome stuff if you can get it to work.'

He doesn't own many bitcoins, I discover. I ask him why.

'From an economic perspective I don't like Bitcoin too much. I don't think it's a viable currency. Generally money has three components. It's a store of value, a means of exchange and a unit of account. And you need all three for it to actually be real money. And then of course there are a lot of properties that you generally look at to determine if it's high quality money or not. So you look at things like the visibility, ease of transferability, how the scarcity dynamics of the money work. You look at the range of products and services that you can acquire for that token. You also look at the groups of people who have control over the supply-and-demand dynamics.

'From the perspective of being good money, Bitcoin fails the unit of account property because we don't natively price products and services with Bitcoin. Rather we look to a fiat standard like the US dollar and we convert the value of the Bitcoin to actually price goods and services. The argument people tend to use is that, well, it's still a small economy, if it got really large people would price things with it.

'The other problem is that I don't think there's ever going to be price stability with Bitcoin.

'First, there are a lot of innovative pressures. There's tons of competition, there's over 300 altcoins and there's always new technology being invented. So that does have a very significant effect on the price of Bitcoin.

'Second, we have rapid demand changes. Suddenly there are loads of buyers, everyone wants to get into Bitcoin, then just as suddenly they don't. It's very volatile.

'Third, the ownership distribution of Bitcoin – about 50 people seem to control half of all the bitcoins because of early-adopter effect. It behaves much more like a tech stock or a commodity from that perspective than it does like a currency.

'That said, it is really interesting that someone has basically been able to create a decentralized digital currency – I should say "commodity" – that could be used as a proto-money. That's a humongous accomplishment.'

Why has he got involved, then?

'From a cryptographic standpoint, what's fascinating about Bitcoin is the identity management component and the block chain technology. The cryptographic problem known as authentication is what got me interested in the space. We've been studying authentication for about 23 years, 24 years in the cryptographic community. The idea is, how do I know you are who you say you are over something like the internet? If I meet you in person I can authenticate by your face and your voice and your mannerisms and so forth, but if I meet you over email or over chat or you're logging into a server, how do I actually know you're really Dominic versus Charles or William or some malfeasant actor?

'Generally this is accomplished by some sort of authentication scheme like usernames or passwords, but those are imperfect and clunky. I think that the technology of Bitcoin, the block chain itself, can actually become a God-send for a next generation ID system that could inevitably get rid of passwords and get rid of usernames and allow people to better authenticate themselves on the internet.

'And once you have that foundation built, you've actually built secure NSA-proof communications systems. You can build new types of ecommerce systems, you can do a whole bunch of really interesting things that you couldn't do before. And it's a global standard, so it doesn't mean you have to win the geographic lottery and live in England or the United States to get a good credit system or good ID system. This is a system that would work just as well in Africa as it works in North America or Europe, which is a huge step forward for ecommerce and banking the unbanked. And that's what gets me really excited about the technology and why I came into this space.'

So, what exactly is Ethereum? Everybody's talking about it, but few seem to understand it.

'Ethereum is really a continuation of what Satoshi Nakamoto was working on. He wanted to study two things when he released Bitcoin. He'd been working on it for quite some time. The first was this idea of a decentralized database secured by a proof-of-work consensus system, and the second thing was a transaction system – tokens. He wanted to see if the consensus system would be cryptographically secure and if people would actually participate in securing it, and, secondly, if the tokens would achieve any market value without any backing or promises. In both cases it was wildly successful.

'He had a third option. You could have programmable money *and* you could have programmable smart contracts that extended Bitcoin into something beyond just a money system – into a kind of a replacement for the current way the internet works. But he felt that there were a lot of concerns from scalability to security, so he purposefully neutered the scripting language of Bitcoin, so as to not enable this. We call it state and Turing completeness.

'So, it's been five years, we've learned a huge amount of lessons, there's been a lot of overlay protocols, other attempts to increase the functionality of Bitcoin. What we did with Ethereum is we kind of unified a lot of the 2.0 actors and put them into a big bucket and we're building a completely new block chain and we're building a completely new scripting language that basically adds in those missing features.

'The end result is you can do things now like have Wall Street on a block chain. So any financial contract that you would see in Wall Street can now be put on a block chain just like money can. You can do prediction markets. You can have a Las Vegas gambling system living on a block chain. You can also take traditional server client internet apps like YouTube or Facebook or Netflix and you can actually now make all of these services run in a decentralized way with no central actor controlling them. You can do decentralized Dropbox, so instead of having all your files stored on a server; you can actually store them in a decentralized network and instead provide them with a token system just like Bitcoin. That's what we're working on to do with Ethereum.

'Bitcoin was an exploration of how can we build a decentralized value system. And if you want to call it money, call it money – but a decentralized money system where we dis-intermediate the government from the generation of money, okay. Ethereum is extracting that and saying what else can we dis-intermediate? Can we remove Dropbox from storage? Can we remove Rackspace and Amazon from hosting? Can we remove Las Vegas from gambling? Can we remove Wall Street from finance? And instead can we run these things in a decentralized way?

'It's a continuation of that experiment and we're seeing how many other things in society we can actually decentralize in nature so that they're not controlled by any one actor. We want to let people choose and program whatever disintermediation they want.'

It's revolutionary stuff. The implications to existing internet business models are substantial. What kind of progress has been made?

'We came up with the idea back in November of last year, there was a white paper drafted by a gentleman named Vitalik Buterin, who is the co-founder of *Bitcoin Magazine* and a pretty big figure in the space. And since then we've released five proof of concepts and we're just about ready to begin a sale to fund the project's development. We anticipate releasing our block chain in the fourth quarter of this year.

'It's very complex. And we haven't done a great job at trying to sell that to the mainstream, because we're still trying to figure out the base technology. There's a lot of work to do to figure out the scripting language and we have to make sure it scales and we have to get developers to build apps. But in the coming months we're going to really start outreaching to people and our goal is to actually unify the whole space behind something called the ether browser.

'Our vision at the end of the year is that you're going to be able to download a piece of software that's kind of like the android of the crypto-currency space, where everything that you wanted to do is one-click installation. So you download a single app and then you'll have an app catalogue, and your wallet is one-click installation, any coin you want to use – it's one click. You can even create your own currency with one click. Your identity management system for NSA-proof communication, that's one click installation and so forth. And if people want to create their own apps, they can do that. And they can do it in a matter of days, if not weeks.

'And so that's our hope, that's what we want to do. And the app catalogue is totally decentralized just like the network. So even we don't control it – so we can't take apps down or anything and the government can't take apps down or something like that. So, that's what we're trying to do: mainstream this dis-intermediation technology'.

The implications of Ethereum – if it takes off – are clearly enormous.

For more information about Ethereum, visit ethereum.org.

# 10

# SHOULD YOU BUY IN?

*You can't stop things like Bitcoin. It's like trying to stop*
*gunpowder. It will be everywhere and the world will*
*have to readjust.*

— John McAfee, computer scientist, founder of McAfee Inc

In the 1830s and 1840s a mania gripped the UK.

A similar mania would soon grip the US in the 1870s and again in the 1890s.

It was about a new technology, a technology that was changing the world: rail transport.

By the late 1830s all the conditions were in place for a frenzy. The Liverpool and Manchester railway had proved a success, the Bank of England had cut interest rates, the Industrial Revolution had created a new, wealthy middle-class and the new medium of newspapers meant that companies could advertise themselves and news could travel quickly. There was an overriding belief in this revolutionary technology and there was money to invest. Railway mania was born.

Hundreds of railway companies sprung up and investment poured in. Land was bought, tracks were laid and trains were built.

But it soon became clear that railways were not as easy to build as was once thought, nor was it so easy to turn a profit. Many of the companies were unviable. Some of them were get-rich-quick schemes and scams.

Then, in 1845, the Bank of England put up interest rates. Capital flowed out of railways and into the bond market instead. New railway investment dried up. As they were still unprofitable, most of the companies went bust. But a few well-capitalized companies, such as Great Western and Midland, were able to pick up the pieces – buying up the tracks, for example, for a fraction of what it had cost to build them.

Some of those large companies still exist today in one form or another. Trains still pass on the railways that were laid nearly 200 years ago. But almost all of the early investors lost their shirts.

All new technology seems to go through a similar cycle.

Take dotcom stocks at the end of the 20th century. Speculators were right: the internet did change the world. They still lost their money.

Most of those dotcom start-ups never made it. Just a handful survived the mania – the likes of Google, Amazon and eBay – and they grew to dominate the space. It is 2014 and the Nasdaq (where most internet stocks are listed) is *still* trading below its 2000 high.

In the 1930s there were as many as 600 American car companies. Now there are three.

I have argued that the technology of Bitcoin is not only here to stay, but that it is going to change the world – just as railways, cars and the internet did. Fortunes will be made – that I do not doubt.

But, counter-intuitive though it may seem, that doesn't mean you should speculate. As with the dotcom boom of the late 1990s and early 2000s, many of the companies now operating in the Bitcoin space, including most of the altcoins that have sprung up, will amount to nothing.

There might be computer geniuses at the helm, but conceiving and implementing a good idea and running a successful company are two very different skills – the latter requires considerable experience that many people do not have. As an investor, successfully identifying the future Googles, Amazons and eBays from the plethora of Boos, Beenz and Flooz is no easy task – even if you know what you're doing. Often, what seem like bad ideas turn out to be good ones, while good ones don't make it if their timing is slightly out.

My advice is have a bit of fun and put some speculative capital to work. By all means, research Bitcoin companies or find a fund that will do the homework for you, though at this stage most funds are still private. Buy some coins – but go in with your eyes wide open. The lesson of history is clear: even with technology that changes the way we do things, you will still probably lose money. Only a handful of the companies and altcoins that have sprung up will make it, but those that do could dominate the space for many years to come, just as those few rail, car and dotcom companies that survived did.

## Beware of the hype cycle

There is a cycle that a new technology passes through as it

goes from conception to widespread adoption. The research company Gartner has dubbed it the 'hype cycle'. It has five phases: the technology trigger, the peak of inflated expectations, the trough of disappointment, the slope of enlightenment and the plateau of productivity.

In the first phase the new technology is invented. There is research and development and some early investment is found. The first products are brought to market. They are expensive and will need a lot of improvement, but they find some early users. The technology clearly has something special about it and people start getting excited. This is the 'technology trigger'. The internet in the early 1990s is a good example.

As this excitement grows, we move into the second phase. The media start talking about this amazing new technology. Speculative money piles in. All sorts of new companies spring up to operate in this new sector. Many of them are just chasing hot money and have no real product to offer. They are sometimes fraudulent. This new technology is going to change the world. The possibilities are endless. We're going to cure diseases. We're going to solve energy problems. We're going to build houses on the moon. This is the 'peak of inflated expectations'. This was the internet in 2000.

But at some point, the needle of reality punctures the bubble of expectation, and we move into the third phase. Actually, this technology might not be quite as good as we thought it was; it's going to take a lot of work to get it right and to make it succeed on a commercial scale. A great deal of not particularly rewarding hard work, time and investment lies ahead. Forget the ideas men – now we need the water-carriers. Suddenly, the excitement has gone.

Negative press starts to creep in. Now there are more sellers than buyers. Investment is harder to come by. Many companies start going bust. People are losing money. The hype cycle has reversed and we have descended into the 'trough of disappointment.' This was the internet between 2000 and 2003.

But now that the hot money has left, we can move into phase four. The incompetent or fraudulent companies have died. The sector has been purged. Most of those that remain are serious players. Investors now demand better practice and the survivors deliver it. They release the second and third generation products, and they work quite well. More and more people start to use the technology and it is finally finding mainstream adoption. This was the internet in 2004. It climbed the 'Slope of Enlightenment', the fourth phase of the hype cycle, and entered the 'Plateau of Productivity' – phase five – which is where the likes of Google, Amazon and eBay are today.

Of course, cycles like this are arbitrary. Reality is never quite so simple. But it's easy to make the case that crypto-currencies in late 2013 reached a 'peak of inflated expectations'.

Perhaps it was not *the* peak. It wasn't Bitcoin's dotcom 2000 moment – just a peak on a larger journey up. Many Bitcoin companies, for example, are not even listed on the stock market. Greater manias could lie ahead.

But it's also easy to make the case that it was *the* peak of inflated expectations. In the space of three or four years, Bitcoin went from an understated mention on an obscure mailing list to declarations that it was not only going to become the preferred money system of the world, but also the usurper of the existing world order. At $1,000 a coin, some early adopters had made a million times their original investment. Speculators marvelled at the colossal amount of money they were making. The media were crazy for it. Bitcoin was discussed all over television.

It caught the imagination of the left, the right and the in-between. Computer boffins marvelled at the impossibly resilient code. Economists and libertarians marvelled at the politics of a money without government or border. There were early adopters, from the tech savvy to the black markets (black markets are usually quick to embrace new technology – pornography was the first business sector to actually make money on the internet, for example).

Every Tom, Dick and Harry you met under the age of 30 with an interest in IT was involved in some Bitcoin start-up or other. Either that or he was designing some new alt currency – some altcoins were rising at over a thousand per cent per day. 'Banks, governments, they're irrelevant now,' these upstarts declared.

I suggest that in late 2013 we hit the peak of the hype cycle – the peak of inflated expectations. Now Bitcoin is somewhere in the 'trough of disillusionment,' just like the internet in 2001. The price has fallen. There have been thefts. Some of the companies involved have gone bankrupt.

The challenge now is for all those start-ups to make their product or service work. They have to take Bitcoin from a great idea and a technology that works to something with much wider 'real world' use. They have to find investment and get more and more people to start using the coins. This is a long process.

There are many who will disagree with this interpretation. And, with investment, it is dangerous to have rigid opinions – I reserve the right to change my mind as events unfold.

## You could still make a mint

There seems to be a 100-year cycle in money.

1716 saw the first Great Recoinage, in the years after Isaac Newton had taken over at the Bank of England. A hundred years later, after excess spending on the Napoleonic Wars, there was another Great Recoinage in 1816. 1913-4 saw another fundamental change to the monetary system with the founding of the Federal Reserve Bank in the US and in Europe the move away from the gold standard.

And here we are in 2014-15, a hundred years later, with this new threat to the monetary order that is Bitcoin and the other crypto-currencies that have followed. If they really do take off, despite everything I've just said, you could still make a great deal of money speculating in Bitcoin and altcoins.

Let's imagine Bitcoin becomes an established asset class in itself – along with the likes of gold, commodities, bonds and stocks. I'll give you some blue-sky targets.

Global ecommerce was $1.2 trillion in 2013. If Bitcoin were to grow to 10% of that, you have a figure of $5,714 per bitcoin.[197] That's over a 1000% gain from current prices.

Current global gold holdings are about $7 trillion. If Bitcoin holdings went to 5% of that, the price would be $17,000 per coin – a 3,400% gain.

Current global money supply stands at $250 trillion. If Bitcoin made up just 1% of that, the price would be $119,000 per coin – a 24,000% gain from the current price of $500.

Assuming widespread adoption of cryptocurrencies, the

lesser-known altcoins, if they take off, will rise by a greater magnitude.

When a bubble gets really big, it grows to the size of the US stock market. At the end of the 1970s bull market in gold, the value of global gold holdings exceeded the market cap of the entire US stock market. At the climax of the Japanese bull market of the 1980s, the Japanese stock market matched the US stock market for size. The value of global tech stocks in 2000 did the same.

At present the total market cap of US stocks stands at around $22 trillion. The combined market value of Bitcoin and the altcoins stands at $7.5 billion. If Bitcoin becomes a bubble on the scale of gold in the 1970s, Japan in the 1980s or tech stocks in the 1990s, then gains of 300,000% might be ahead!

I wouldn't hold your breath.

But even so, perhaps it makes sense to open an account with an exchange and risk a small amount of speculative capital on some coins – but only money that you can afford to lose, if there is such a thing. The other alternative is to find some start-ups and put some money to work there – or find a fund that does the same.

But the compelling evidence of history is that you could also lose a lot more than your shirt. Cryptocurrencies could be widow-makers. *Caveat emptor!*

## The next great bull market

In the 1970s, the bull market was gold. It rose from just $35 in 1971 to $850 per ounce in 1980. Gold mining companies increased by many times that.

In the 1980s Japan was the place to be – its companies and its real estate.

In the 1990s dot com stocks were the rage; in the 2000s commodities were.

But what about the 2010s? What is the great bull market of this decade? US stocks, maybe? Biotech, perhaps, or London property?

Well, no. So far it's been Bitcoin. And I think the next phase will be one of its offshoots.

We'll call it block chain tech.

Block chain tech is going to change everything – not just money and banking, but the law, accounting, social media, email, gambling, web hosting, cloud computing, stock markets even. It could be more earth-shattering than the World Wide Web.

As we've seen with Ethereum, now that Bitcoin is up and running, developers are extending the technology of the block chain into all sorts of other applications.

You have Bitmessage – a decentralized system of sending and receiving emails without Google or Hotmail or whoever your email service provider might be having access to your messages. Nobody can read them, except the people you send them to.

You have Twister – like Twitter, but peer-to-peer and with no central body. It's a much safer way to organize an Arab Spring or indulge in the kind of free speech that can get you into trouble.

You can register ownership of financial assets and have contracts verified on a block chain. This has all sorts of implications for Wall Street, the City and the huge business models of share registrars and brokers. Car ownership and land ownership could be registered on a block chain (and in the UK this is not before time. Both the DVLA and the Land Registry badly need to pull their socks up, particularly the latter – 50% of land in the UK is still unregistered). This system of ownership and smart contracts has the potential to dramatically transform the legal system and slash costs.

As we've suggested, insurance can be put on a block chain, prediction markets, and identity systems (username and password systems are on their way out), even services like Facebook, YouTube or Netflix.

Why would you want YouTube, Facebook or Netflix running in a decentralized way with no central body in charge? It eliminates the problem of excessive personal information on Facebook, or your YouTube viewing habits being monitored and marketed to. And think about the copyright implications for the TV and movie industries. How on earth will copyright be enforced with decentralized viewing platforms? Existing business models will have to adapt or die.

Even the American-controlled system of domain name registration, ICANN, for all its non-profit status and good intentions, is under threat from something genuinely independent – the decentralized Namecoin.

The implications are enormous – not just to corporations, but to governments as well. If everything can be dis-intermediated and decentralized, what about the services governments provide – healthcare, welfare and education? The bureaucratic middleman megalith that makes them so inefficient and expensive could be circumvented altogether.

It will even bring into question our system of representative democracy. The tech is there for people's identity to be proven and for them to vote instantly on just about any issue that comes up – gay marriage, abortion law, planning permission, military intervention. Liquid democracy – where people actually vote on decisions as they get made – is surely a far truer democracy. Why then do you need a congressman or parliamentary representative?

In the years ahead a huge battle for control is coming, as those who have been outdated try to cling on.

The revolution will not be televised. It will be time-stamped on the block chain.

It is all very exciting.

For any conventional or mainstream investor, aside from buying altcoins, it is almost too early to buy in. There are no listed companies. There is no block chain tech ETF you can buy. There is no tracker fund (although it is coming – cryptocomposite.com is leading the way there). Almost all of these companies are private and mostly self-funded. Many of them may not ever list on stock markets, at least not in the current conventional way. But this is huge groundbreaking stuff – and investment products will soon become available, of that you can be sure. I'd say we're about where the internet was in 1991. There's still plenty of time to get on board. Perhaps we're at the 'technology trigger' phase of the hype cycle for block chain tech. That phase when investments stratospherically rise to the 'peak of inflated expectations' is still ahead for block chain tech – even if it might not necessarily be for Bitcoin. Bitcoin may be just the beginning of something bigger.

So, keep your eyes and ears peeled – block chain tech is the next great bull market. You heard it here first.

# 11

# THE PEOPLE'S MONEY

*I would be surprised if ten years from now we're not using electronic currency – now that we know a way to do it...*
— Satoshi Nakamoto

I have probably got a little too evangelical about Bitcoin and what it's going to do to the world.

Therein lies one of its many problems. Its champions often do not question it enough – they eulogize instead.

There are a host of problems that Bitcoin will have to overcome.

All new disruptive technologies will face detractors who try to limit their potential. The biggest detractors of all are those who the disruptive tech threatens to undermine. In this case, we're talking about resistance from the two most powerful sectors of society – government and finance. Who knows what kinds of reactionary regulation could be round the corner if Bitcoin grows? To what extent will banks lobby governments to stop it somehow?

The next big issue is that its user base is still too small. As the number of users grows, it will meet with increasing pressure from its detractors.

Its price volatility might mean speculators like it, but, again, ordinary users will not. This volatility may settle over time. But there's no guarantee of that. Until it does, mainstream adoption will be a problem.

Its mobile platform support – or lack thereof – is also standing in the way of mainstream adoption. Apple had taken steps to make sure users cannot send bitcoins via wallets in its app store, though this policy seems to be reversing as this book goes to press. Google does not allow in-app payments. It's not clear why either has done this, but it's thought the reason is fear of falling foul of US government regulation.

Another mainstream adoption problem is that Bitcoin's ownership is too concentrated among early-adopters. Approximately 50 people are believed to own half of all bitcoins, and a handful of companies dominate bitcoin mining. Ironically, this has, in a way, made Bitcoin centralized. These coins need to be disseminated somehow. Higher prices should fix that problem.

There are still too many bad actors and too many opportunities for cons, hacks and other crimes. Its widespread usership in black markets could undermine it – and certainly increase the likelihood of government opposition.

Then there is the theoretical question of what it is – a medium of exchange, a store of wealth or a new asset class? People still think in terms of dollars and pounds rather than bitcoins. They price things in dollars. They don't think about how many bitcoins they're going to own. They think about how many dollars they're eventually going to get for their bitcoins.

Bitcoin is a breakthrough tech. Now that the floodgates

have been opened, it could quickly be undermined by something that is better. Who uses Sony Walkmans or Amstrad home computers now?

Time may cure many of these problems – particularly the issue of widespread adoption. We shall see.

But let us end on a positive note.

## Truth in numbers - in each other we trust

It is a wonderful thing that, after decades of ignorance, Bitcoin has got people talking about money systems once again – and, more importantly, questioning them.

I'm a fervent believer that many of Western society's problems lie in our flawed system of money – not least, this awful and widening gap between rich and poor. Changing our system of money wouldn't solve everything overnight, of course not, but it would be the points on the railway – the railway switch – that re-route the unstoppable, runaway train that Western society has become. I've written a whole book about it – *Life After the State* – so it's inevitable that Bitcoin and the cryptos are going to appeal to me.

But Bitcoin is an incredibly multi-faceted creation that means many different things to different people. It has so many implications for the world. That's what makes it controversial. That's what gets it discussed. And that's what gives it power.

So, what exactly is Bitcoin?

Bitcoin is a means to an end.

It is a way to involve billions in the world economy.

If you're one of the unbanked, or 'under banked' – an adolescent, a citizen of a Third World country, or even a vagrant, Bitcoin enables you to participate in ecommerce avoiding the barriers the current banking system puts up.

If you use the internet at all, you can make payment to and receive payment from anyone anywhere, even for a tiny amount. It will open up whole new markets. It saves on fees, increases speed of payment and, no matter where they live, enables people to appeal and gain access to a sophisticated, tech-savvy demographic with a substantial disposable income.

It is a way to protect.

If you live in a country with an over-leveraged, vulnerable banking sector (Cyprus, for example), with a poor record of inflation, capital controls or confiscation (Argentina, Zimbabwe, Romania are just three of many), or with crippling levels of taxation or regulation, now you can escape local banking and money systems.

You might not like having to hand over your financial details to and then rely on the security practices of people you buy things from. You might not like organizations knowing about your spending habits, or being marketed things based on these habits. Bitcoin protects your financial information and your privacy.

If you want to send money to friends and family back home, you can do so shielded from the costliness and clumsness of current systems.

And, yes, if you operate on the wrong side of the law, it is a safer way than fiat currencies to buy and sell illegal goods.

It is a way to progress.

If you're an innovator or an entrepreneur, you can fund new ideas without having to rely on traditional systems or the endorsement of large, slow-moving financial institutions.

If you're a speculator, it's a means to get rich (or poor) quickly. If you're in business, here is a new efficient way to communicate, to prove ownership and write contracts. If you're in technology, here is a fascinating new application – a watershed – that opens up a myriad of new possibilities.

If you have an interest in economics, here is an opportunity to experience and study what is possibly a paradigm shift, taking place in real time in the real world around us – private and non-national currencies competing with government currencies, as economist Friedrich Hayek advocated in his seminal 1976 paper, *The Denationalization of Money*.

It is a way to change to the world.

If you're an activist, here is an organic way to redistribute wealth through society and bypass existing corporate monopolies. If you're a libertarian or an anarchist, here is a way to escape the clutches of government and its crony banks. If you're a computer scientist or an entrepreneur, here is a new tech that has as much disruptive potential as the internet. And, if you're a revolutionary, here is a way to overthrow the existing world order.

All in all, Bitcoin is quite something.

The block chain – a mere database in the eyes of some – is perhaps the most fantastically subversive technology ever invented.

# Appendix I:
# A Beginner's Guide to
# Buying Bitcoins

There are three ways to get hold of bitcoins.

You can either buy them, earn them or mine them.

I would suggest beginners ignore mining for the time being. Mining has become a specialized endeavour that takes a bit of experience and a lot of computer power. Earn them or buy them instead.

The first thing you will need is a wallet. The simplest place to get one of these is blockchain.info. Click on 'Wallet' and you'll have one as quickly as you can type in your email address and password.

Once you have a wallet, you have an address – a place to receive your bitcoins.

If you want to earn coins, simply mention that you accept bitcoins wherever you advertise your goods or services and add the option to pay with Bitcoin at your point of sale. So, if you have a website, have your web designer add a Bitcoin button and a payment function. If you have a shop, keep some means to accept bitcoins by the tills. If you send out invoices, put your wallet address on the invoice. It'll take a few goes before you get comfortable with it – but it really is very simple, and it's also fun practising something new. Often, the person you are trading with will know a bit more than you and they'll actually help you get to grips with it.

Now we come to actually buying bitcoins.

The simplest way is to open an account with a recognized exchange, deposit some money and then use that money to buy some coins. What's the best exchange? Coinbase, Bitstamp and Bittylicious are three names to think about, though that is not a recommendation. The best exchange for you will vary according to which country you are in, but make sure you go for one that is legitimate. You might have to do a bit of homework.

Another method is to try localbitcoins.com. This site will put you in touch with local sellers and you can often buy bitcoins for cash. Make sure you choose a trader with a good reputation (each seller will have user reviews by their name). In many cases, you can actually meet up with the seller – which can work well as you're bound to be able to learn something from them. But don't do this with large volumes of cash, unless you have done proper due diligence.

Another simple way to buy bitcoins with cash is via one of the ATMs, which are gradually springing up in cities around the world.

This is a fast-changing marketplace. Anything I write here will probably be out of date in a few months. To stay current, I would recommend the Bitcoin wiki page – https://en.bitcoin.it/wiki/Buying_Bitcoins (the newbie version) – as Bitcoin users constantly update this. Have a read of it and you'll discover a way to buy coins that suits you. But, however you do it, I would recommend only using small amounts of money at first while you are finding your feet.

As for other useful Bitcoin sites, Coindesk.com – which dubs itself 'the voice of digital currency' – is the best way to stay abreast with Bitcoin news and current affairs. It also has a host of useful data and information (I get the daily email digest). Bitcointalk.org is the biggest forum – a good place to get opinions and stories (as well as all the usual misinformation you find on chat boards).

Coinmarketcap.com is a useful site to introduce yourself to the altcoins. It gives you price information about the hundred biggest cryptocurrencies, as well links to their sites.

For those with an interest in finance, I would also single out cryptocomposite.com. Its CC10 Index measures the performance of the top ten cryptocurrencies in real time. It's almost certain to become the benchmark when tracker funds, ETFs and other financial vehicles eventually arrive to play the price of cryptocurrencies.

As for vehicles to invest in block chain tech, they are coming – of that you can be sure – but they have not yet arrived. As this book goes to press, Ehereum is accepting investment – but you need bitcoins to invest. DigitalBTC is listing on the Australian Stock Exchange. This is the first Bitcoin company to trade on a major stock exchange. It will not be the last. Go to conferences, make as many contacts as you can, read your Coinbase and your Bitcointalk – keep your finger on the pulse.

Enjoy the ride!

# Appendix II:
# Who Is Satoshi? The
# Usual Suspects

*Who is John Galt?*

— Ayn Rand, Atlas Shrugged

There are many names that have bandied about in the fruit-less search for Satoshi. Here – in addition to those in the main chapter – we look at some of the other usual suspects.

Jed McCaleb is one. McCaleb, an entrepreneur, says he first heard about Bitcoin in July 2010 when it was mentioned on Slashdot. He had been involved in a similar idea – Open-Coin – that was hatched at around the same time as Bitcoin in 2008.

There was no easy way to buy bitcoins, so he turned the MtGox domain he had lying about into a Bitcoin exchange. In 2011 he would then sell it, not wanting the day-to-day has-sles of running something so administratively burdensome. He says it wasn't 'technically interesting and I had no interest in running it long-term'.[198]

'I love Bitcoin', he said. 'But the mining process has always bothered me because it wastes so much energy'.[199] This process is something Satoshi had always defended

217

staunchly, arguing that bitcoins should have a cost of production to give them value and that this cost is more than justified by the efficiencies it creates elsewhere. This essential contradiction in their point of view of what is a key building block of Bitcoin makes it unlikely that Satoshi and McCaleb are the same person.

In addition, McCaleb's early MtGox's encryption of passwords was amateur, irresponsible even. It endangered users, violating basic guidelines that Satoshi would surely have known.

McCaleb would go on to start another cryptocurrency – Ripple. As he was doing so, he advertised on BitcoinTalk for a C++ coder.[200] If he were Satoshi, he probably wouldn't have needed one.

He has since left Ripple and begun work on another Bitcoin project.

It's also worth noting that, soon after joining the BitcoinTalk forums, he asked some fairly basic questions about Bitcoin in a prose that is not as precise as Satoshi's.

There are parallels, no doubt. McCaleb has a history of developing peer-to-peer sharing sites, running on the edge of the law. He had an interest in digital cash. But his tendency to build something, sell it and move on suggests to me he doesn't have Satoshi's patience, nor would he have hoarded the bitcoins in the way that Satoshi has. He would, more probably, have sold some of them (as he has with his Ripples), but I have no proof of that.

Mark Karpelès, whose Tokyo-based company Tibanne bought MtGox from McCaleb, has also been suggested. There is that same Japanese connection. The fiasco that

MtGox would become is surely evidence enough that he was no Satoshi.

The most vulnerable point of the Bitcoin set-up is the point of transference from fiat to bitcoin. Given Satoshi's foresight, and his knowledge of the way authorities work, we can comfortably assume that an exchange and all the associated headaches is not something he would have wanted to get involved with. Why would anyone who values his privacy as much as Satoshi place himself in such a conspicuous position? It's not like he needed the money.

Paco Ahlgren is a libertarian author and financial analyst whose name was also thrown into the hat. He denied any connection. He doesn't have the coding skills, is much more overt in his politics than Satoshi and, as an author selling books, is considerably more avid for publicity.

The broadcaster Max Keiser is another whose name has appeared. The broadcaster has been a prominent champion of Bitcoin, but, again, he does not have the coding skills. He is also more outspoken. While Satoshi was working on Bitcoin, Keiser was making TV programmes. There isn't time for both.

Amazingly, there is even an argument that Satoshi was Ross Ulbricht. What are these people smoking?

Would Satoshi risk everything he stands to gain by creating the de facto digital cash system on an illegal venture like the Silk Road? Satoshi was more meticulous than Ulbricht – he never accidentally left his real name and email on a website or ordered forged documents to be sent to his home address.

And, of course, Satoshi was more understated in his politics than Ulbricht and the Dread Pirate Roberts. They might both have shared the same views, but Ulbricht/the Dread Pirate Roberts were both much more vocal.

Gavin Andresen, the great coder, who would replace Martti Malmi as Bitcoin's number two, has also been suggested. A quick glance at the conversations between the two at BitcoinTalk shows there are clearly two different people talking. In addition, they have different coding styles.

'If you ask a geek to look at some of the code I've written in the past', says Andresen, 'and look at Satoshi's early code, they can tell it is written by two different people, a different writing style. I mean you can tell the difference between a Kurt Vonnegut novel and a Jackie Collins novel, or whatever. And so in the geek world, none of the geeks believe that I'm Satoshi. I mean he likes Hungarian notation for this or that variable and I'm, like, nah.'[201]

Malmi himself is another name that has been ventured. But he is not old enough, in my view, and his English, though excellent, is not as impeccable as Satoshi's. A quick read of his posts reveals this.

The reclusive Japanese-American mathematician Shinichi Mochizuki was a hot favourite to be Satoshi at one stage, thanks to a YouTube video released by the outspoken Californian academic, Ted Nelson. Mochizuki made no public denial. He certainly has the writing and mathematical ability, but there is no evidence of his having the C++ coding skills, nor the background in cryptography or Cypherpunk, let alone the interest or desire to devise an electronic currency. He's all about the maths. The plethora of academic papers he released during the 2007–10 period that Satoshi was developing Bitcoin indicates he would also not have had the time for Bitcoin.

The Munich-based trio Neal J King, Charles Bry and Vladimir Oksman were brought into the fray as a result of a patent they filed a few days before the Bitcoin website was registered. Professor Penenberg, who was Satoshi-sleuthing for Fast Company, argued that it contained some suspiciously similar terms, including the phrase 'computationally impractical to reverse.' Except their patent actually contained the phrase 'reverse-map', which is different.

Penenberg was also excited by the fact that bitcoin.org was registered in Finland and Charles Fry had travelled to Finland in 2007. The site was registered in Finland for no such reason – it was because Martti Malmi had registered it there. King, Bry and Oksman are a trio – not the one-man band that Satoshi appears to be – they have no background in Cypherpunk culture and their patent was for something very different to Bitcoin.

John Noecker Jr has run stylometrics tests on King, Bry and Oksman, as well as mathematicians Shinichi Mochizuki and Michael Clear, once the *New Yorker*'s favourite man. Noecker found that King was the most likely of all of them. He then ran the same tests on Hal Finney and concluded 'Finney is the most likely of all of them.' And we know Finney is not Satoshi.

Jon Matonis from the Bitcoin Foundation is another suggestion that has been made. Matonis had the vision – he was writing about a digital cash world back in the 1990s, but he doesn't have the coding skills. The author Robert Hettinga, who focuses on financial cryptography, has also been suggested. Hettinga is another one who has the vision, but he is probably too outspoken – and again he doesn't have the coding skills. He also prefers Unix to Windows.

David Chaum, the inventor of Digicash, is another possibility, suggested by Andrew Smith in the *Sunday Times*. I
suspect Chaum may have been too controlling to leave his
product to the open-source community. Nevertheless, in stylometrics tests, which analysed word-length frequency and
character frequency, Chaum ranked as a very low possibility.[202] Moreover, Bitcoin makes little use of Chaum's
ground-breaking blind signatures, which is, as blogger
Gwern writes to me, 'a bit like Newton not using Calculus'.

# Acknowledgements

To everybody who has funded this book, thank you. Your names are in the back for all to see. Without your generosity and interest, this book would never have happened. I am very grateful. In particular, I mention the names of Carl Holt, Brian Cartmell, Duncan Black, Wade Smith, Bill Reid, Antony Ward, Bandish Nayee, Chris Valle, William Bonner, Salim Halabi, Jane Aitken and Paul Fisher.

The world of computer programming and cryptography was new to me six months ago, but I have discovered its inhabitants to be extremely helpful and generous with their time and expertise. Most, but not all of the names that follow are from that world (and some have asked to remain anonymous). For your help in the researching, writing and fact-checking of this book I thank Rob Fischer, Adam Back, Nick Szabo, Amir Taaki, Alessandro Polverini, Wei Dai, Charles Hoskinson, Martti Malmi, Charles Morris, Jonathan James Harrison, Darren Hopkinson, Andy Alness, Seth Roberts, Adam Poulton, John Noeker Jnr, Jesse Lozano, Paul Gordon and Richard Boase.

I would like to thank the Bitcoin and open-source communities for all that you do online. The contribution that people make to the internet every day in terms of the sharing of ideas, information, knowledge and experience make it the most invaluable resource. You have all made Bitcoin happen.

A special thank you is reserved for Toby Bray, CEO of *MoneyWeek*, for your immense editorial contribution: feedback that is always prompt and detailed – despite being extremely busy with other, more lucrative endeavours – strong opinions, useful techniques to help me through the tricky stuff and an exceptional understanding of what people want to read.

Thank you also to the maverick that is Gwern Branwen, another prompt replier, highly intelligent and laconic, for your many suggestions and your eye for detail.

I asked Gwern to read this book for what he does know, I asked my dad for what he doesn't. Aged 82, as computer-illiterate a man as you could ever hope to meet, if Terence Frisby can follow it all, anybody can. Thanks Dad, as ever, for the notes.

I would like to thank everyone at Unbound – in particular editor Isobel Frankish, Caitlin Harvey, Dan Kieran, Baldur Bjarnason, Xander Cansell, Charlie Gleason, Rachael Kerr, Cathy Hurren and Fiona Dempsey. A special mention must be saved for Tim Mahar for so respectfully smoothing over a rough situation, for copy editor Sarah Chamberlain and for the indefatigable Jane Beaton in charge of PR.

I thank Adrian Sear of Soundtracks for recording and mixing the audiobook. What a sound engineer you are. I also thank social networking expert Jimmy Leach because I so rudely didn't thank him properly for *Life After the State*. And I thank Tamsin Rickeard for her invaluable help – I haven't forgotten.

Last, but not least I thank Satoshi Nakamoto. You have given the world something special.

# Bibliography

There are various websites I have returned to repeatedly. These are:

Bitcoin Wiki – bitcoin.it/wiki

BitcoinTalk – bitcointalk.org

Coindesk – coindesk.com

Cryptography Mailing List – mail-archive.com/
cryptography@metzdowd.com

Forbes – forbes.com

P2P Foundation – http://bit.ly/1tHF7KA

Reddit – reddit.com

Sourceforge – sourceforge.net

Nick Szabo's Essays, Papers and Concise Tutorials –
szabo.best.vwh.net/

Unenumerated – unenumerated.blogspot.com

'All About Bitcoin.' *Top of Mind* 21. Goldman Sachs. March 11, 2014.
http://bit.ly/1tHF8hR

'Anonymous Speech.' June 16, 2014. http://bit.ly/1tHF8hQ.

Bank of England. *Bank of England Statistical Release*. 30 Jan. 2014.
Web. http://bit.ly/1tHF7KB.

Bank of England. *Money Creation in the Modern Economy*. By Michael
McLeay, Amar Radia, and Ryland Thomas. Bank of England
Quarterly Bulletin, 2014. Web. http://bit.ly/1tHF8y4.

Berkman, Fran. 'Alleged Silk Road mastermind was a dirty hippie, best friend says.' *Mashable*. November 4, 2013. Accessed June 16, 2014. http://on.mash.to/1tHF8y5.

'Bitcoin Forum.' *Bitcoin Forum – Index*. Accessed June 16, 2014. http://bit.ly/1tHF7KI.

'Bitcoin? Here's What Warren Buffett Is Saying.' *CNBC*. March 14, 2013. Accessed June 16, 2014. http://cnb.cx/1tHF7KJ.

'Bitcoin Project Milestones'. *Bitcoin Project Milestones*. Tiki Toki. Accessed June 16, 2014. http://bit.ly/1tHF8y6.

'Bitcoin Wiki.' *Bitcoin*. Accessed June 16, 2014. http://bit.ly/1tHF7KK.

'BitcoinTalk.' *BitcoinTalk.com*. Accessed June 16, 2014. http://bit.ly/1tHF8y8.

Branwen, Gwern. 'Bitcoin – worse is better.' *Gwern.net*. July 20, 2010. http://bit.ly/1tHF7KL.

Branwen, Gwern. 'Silk Road: theory & practice.' *Gwern.net*. June 2011. http://bit.ly/1tHF8y9.

Brito, Jerry. 'Online cash Bitcoin could challenge governments, banks.' *Time*. April 16, 2011. Accessed June 16, 2014. http://ti.me/1tHF7KM.

Casey, Michael J. 'Bitcoin Foundation's Andresen on working with Satoshi Nakamoto.' *MoneyBeat – Wall Street Journal*. March 6, 2014. Accessed June 16, 2014. http://on.wsj.com/1tHF8yc.

'Cell phones could "completely change the livelihood of many Kenyans".' *NBC News*. April 10, 2014. Accessed June 16, 2014. http://nbcnews.to/1tHFaGc.

Chaum, David. *Blind Signatures for Untraceable Payments* (1982). Accessed February 13, 2014. http://bit.ly/1tHFaGd.

Chaves Echeverri, Juan M. 'The global financial tsunami: 2008.' *Lingnan Journal of Banking, Finance and Economics*. 2012. Accessed June 16, 2014. http://bit.ly/1tHFaGe.

Colao, JJ. 'With 60 million websites, WordPress rules the web. So where's the money?" September 5, 2012. http://onforb.es/1tHF8yd.

Connor, Steve. 'Flu epidemic traced to Great War transit camp.' *Irish Independent*. January 8, 2000. Accessed February 11, 2014. http://bit.ly/1tHF8yf.

Cox, James. *Bitcoin and Digital Currencies: The New World of Money and Freedom*. Baltimore: Laissez Faire, 2013.

'Credit card ownership statistics.' *Statistic Brain RSS*. July 24, 2012. Accessed June 16, 2014. http://bit.ly/1tHFaGg.

'Cryptography Mailing List archives.' http://bit.ly/1tHF8yj.

Dai, Wei. 'Wei Dai comments on AALWA: ask any Less Wronger anything.' *Less Wrong*. March 25, 2014. Accessed June 16, 2014. http://bit.ly/1tHFaGj.

Davis, Joshua. 'The crypto-currency.' *New Yorker*. October 10 2011.

Demirguc-Kunt, Asli, and Leora Klapper. 'Measuring financial inclusion.' *World Bank*. April 1, 2012. http://bit.ly/1tHFaGk.

Durden, Tyler. 'JPMorgan on the inevitability of Europe-wide capital controls.' *Zero Hedge*. March 22 2013. Accessed June 16, 2014. http://bit.ly/1tHFaGl.

Financial Action Taskforce, US Federal Bureau of Investigation. *Money Laundering Using New Payment Methods*. October 2010. http://bit.ly/1tHFaGm.

'Find, Create, and Publish Open Source Software for Free.' *Sourceforge*. Accessed June 16, 2014. http://bit.ly/1tHF8yk.

Foley, Stephen. 'Bitcoin needs to learn from past e-currency failures.' *Financial Times*. November 28, 2013. Accessed June 16, 2014. http://on.ft.com/1tHFaGn.

Gilbert, David. 'FBI's Christopher Tarbell – the Elliot Ness of cyberspace who busted Silk Road.' *International Business Times RSS*. October 3, 2013. Accessed June 16, 2014. http://bit.ly/1tHF8yl.

Gladwell, Malcolm. *David and Goliath: The Triumph of the Underdog*. New York: Little, Brown, 2013.

Gladwell, Malcolm. *Outliers: The Story of Success*. New York: Little, Brown, 2008.

Gladwell, Malcolm. *The Tipping Point: How Little Things Can Make a Big Difference*. Boston: Little, Brown, 2000.

Goodman, Leah M. 'The face behind Bitcoin.' *Newsweek*. March 6, 2014. Accessed June 13, 2014. http://bit.ly/1tHFaGp.

Greenberg, Andy. 'Nakamoto's neighbor: my hunt for Bitcoin's creator led to a paralyzed crypto genius.' *Forbes*. March 25, 2014. Accessed June 16, 2014. http://onforb.es/1tHF8ym.

Greenberg, Andy. *This Machine Kills Secrets: How WikiLeakers, Cypherpunks and Hacktivists Aim to Free the World's Information*. New York: Dutton, 2012.

Grey, Skye. 'Occam's razor: who is most likely to be Satoshi Nakamoto?." *Like In A Mirror*. March 11, 2014. Accessed June 16, 2014. http://bit.ly/1tHFaGq.

Hayek, Friedrich A. *Denationalisation of Money: The Argument Refined*. London: London Publishing Partnership, 1976.

Hill, Kashmir. *Secret Money: Living On Bitcoin In The Real World*. Forbes Media, 2014. Ebook. http://onforb.es/1tHFaGr.

'How Currency Gets into Circulation.' Federal Reserve Bank of New York. February 7, 2014. Accessed June 16, 2014. http://nyfed.org/1tHF8OC.

Hughes, Eric. 'A cypherpunk's manifesto.' March 1993. Accessed June 16, 2014. http://bit.ly/1tHFaGs.

'Interview with Jed McCaleb, inventor of the Ripple protocol and co-founder of OpenCoin.' *Ripple*. April 17, 2013. Accessed June 16, 2014. http://bit.ly/1tHF8OD.

Jain, Sudeep. 'Why so few Indians have bank accounts.' *Wall Street*

*Journal India*. November 1, 2012. Accessed June 16, 2014. http://on.wsj.com/1tHFaGt.

Kaminsky, Dan. 'I tried hacking Bitcoin and I failed.' *Business Insider*. April 12, 2013. Accessed June 16, 2014. http://read.bi/1tHF8OE.

Kushner, David. 'Dead end on Silk Road: internet crime kingpin Ross Ulbricht's big fall.' *Rolling Stone*. February 4, 2014. Accessed June 16, 2014. http://rol.st/1tHFaGu.

Laird, Nick. 'ShareLynx charts.' *ShareLynx Gold Charts*. Accessed June 16, 2014. http://bit.ly/1tHF8OF.

Lamport, Leslie, Robert Shostak, and Marshall Pease. 'The Byzantine generals problem.' *SRI International* April 1980. http://bit.ly/1tHFaGv.

Lons, Rob. 'A complete, interactive history of Bitcoin.' *Mashable*. February 10, 2014. Accessed June 16, 2014. http://on.mash.to/1tHF8OG.

'M2 Money Stock'. Federal Reserve Bank of St Louis. February 10, 2014. Accessed June 16, 2014. http://bit.ly/1tHF8OH.

May, Tim. 'The Crypto anarchist manifesto.' 1998. Accessed June 16, 2014. http://bit.ly/1tHF8OI.

McNally, Victoria. 'How the heck do you pronounce "doge," anyway?' *GeekoSystem*. February 10, 2014. Accessed June 16, 2014. http://bit.ly/1tHF8OJ.

Nakamoto, Satoshi. 'Bitcoin: a peer-to-peer electronic cash system.' August 31, 2008. Accessed June 16, 2014. http://bit.ly/1tHFaWK.

Nakamoto, Satoshi. 'Bitcoin open source implementation of P2P currency.' *P2P Foundation*. February 11, 2009. Accessed June 16, 2014. http://bit.ly/1tHFaWL.

*National Taxpayers' Union Talks with Milton Friedman*. Professor Milton Friedman and John Berthoud. YouTube. Spring 1999. Posted August 9, 2012. http://bit.ly/1tHF8OK.

'Number of credit card holders fell in India: HSBC survey.' *Hindu*

*Business Line*. May 13, 2013. Accessed March 20, 2014. http://bit.ly/1tHFaWP.

O'Neill, Patrick H. 'How big is the internet's most notorious black market?' *The Daily Dot*. July 30, 2013. Accessed June 16, 2014. http://bit.ly/1tHF8ON.

Paulson, Henry M. *On the Brink: Inside the Race to Stop the Collapse of the Global Financial System*. New York: Business Plus, 2010.

Peck, Morgan E. 'Bitcoin: the cryptoanarchists' answer to cash.' *IEEE Spectrum*. May 10, 2014. Accessed June 16, 2014. http://bit.ly/1tHFaWR.

Penenberg, Adam L. 'The Bitcoin crypto-currency mystery reopened.' *Fast Company*. October 11, 2011. Accessed June 16, 2014. http://bit.ly/1tHF8OR.

Peston, Robert. 'Bitcoin's life-or-death moment'. BBC News. February 25, 2014. Accessed June 16, 2014. http://bbc.in/1tHF8OS.

'Reddit'. *Reddit: The Front Page of the Internet*. Accessed June 15, 2014. http://bit.ly/1tHFaWT.

'Researchers uncover likely author of original Bitcoin paper.' Aston University. April 16, 2014. Accessed June 16, 2014. http://bit.ly/1tHFaWU.

Regel, Edwin C. *The New Approach to Freedom: Together with Essays on the Separation of Money and State*. San Pedro, CA: Heather Foundation, 2003. http://bit.ly/1tHF956.

'Russian authorities say Bitcoin illegal.' Thomson Reuters. February 9, 2014. Accessed June 16, 2014. http://reut.rs/1tHFaWV.

Smith, Andrew. 'Desperately seeking Satoshi.' *The Sunday Times*. March 2, 2014.

Southurst, Jon. 'Why China is leading the global rise of Bitcoin.' *CoinDesk RSS*. November 18, 2013. Accessed June 16, 2014. http://bit.ly/1tHF957.

Standard, Liberty. 'Exchange rates 2009.' *New Liberty Standard –*

*An Economic Revolution.* Accessed June 16, 2014. http://bit.ly/1tHFaWW.

Stephenson, Neal. *Cryptonomicon.* New York: Avon, 1999.

Szabo, Nicholas. 'Ben Bernanke plays John Law.' Unenumerated. May 13, 2008. Accessed June 16, 2014. http://bit.ly/1tHFaXo.

Szabo, Nicholas. 'Bit gold markets.' Unenumerated. April 8, 2008. Accessed June 16, 2014. http://bit.ly/1tHF95b.

Szabo, Nicholas. 'Bitcoin – what took ye so long?'. Unenumerated. May 28, 2011. Accessed June 16, 2014. http://bit.ly/1tHFbde.

Szabo, Nicholas. 'Bit gold.' Unenumerated. December 29, 2005 Accessed March 30, 2014. http://bit.ly/1tHF95d.

Szabo, Nicholas. 'Consulting services.' Unenumerated. April 2, 2008. Accessed June 16, 2014. http://bit.ly/1tHF95e.

Szabo, Nicholas. 'Contracts with Bearer.' Nick Szabo's Essays, Papers, and Concise Tutorials. March 12, 2008. Accessed June 16, 2014. http://bit.ly/1tHFbdj.

Szabo, Nicholas. 'Flying money.' Unenumerated. August 27, 2008. Accessed June 16, 2014. http://bit.ly/1tHF95h.

Szabo, Nicholas. 'How to protect your electronic privacy.' April 27, 1993. Accessed June 16, 2014. http://bit.ly/1tHFbdn.

Szabo, Nicholas. 'New Zealander challenges Amazon one-click patent.' Unenumerated. December 20, 2005. Accessed June 16, 2014. http://bit.ly/1tHF95j.

Szabo, Nicholas. 'Shelling out – the origins of money.' Shelling Out – The Origins of Money. 2002. Accessed June 16, 2014. http://bit.ly/1tHFbdp.

Szabo, Nicholas. 'Ten ways to make a political difference'. Unenumerated. August 12, 2007. Accessed June 16, 2014. http://bit.ly/1tHF95l.

Szabo, Nick. 'Antiques, time, gold and bit gold.' Unenumerated. August 28, 2008. Accessed June 16, 2014. http://bit.ly/1tHFbdq.

Taylor, Adam. 'Alleged founder of Silk Road posted LinkedIn manifesto about using economic theory to change the world.' *Business Insider*. October 2, 2013. Accessed June 16, 2014. http://j.mp/1tHFbds.

Thomas, Keir. 'Could the Wikileaks scandal lead to new virtual currency?' *PCWorld*. December 10, 2012. Accessed June 16, 2014. http://bit.ly/1tHF95n.

Titcomb, James. 'Bitcoin under threat as MtGox goes offline.' *The Telegraph*. Telegraph Media Group, February 25, 2014. Accessed June 16, 2014. http://bit.ly/1tHF9lC.

Treanor, Jill, Wintour, Patrick and Ashley Seager. 'Staring into the abyss.' *Guardian*. October 9, 2008. Accessed June 16, 2014. http://bit.ly/1tHF9lF.

Worstall, Tim. 'Finally, a proper use for Bitcoin, avoiding capital controls.' *Forbes*. November 21, 2013. Accessed June 16, 2014. http://onforb.es/1tHFbtQ.

Yeoman, Kyla. 'M-Pesa helps world's poorest go to the bank using mobile phones.' *The Christian Science Monitor*. January 6, 2014. Accessed June 16, 2014. http://bit.ly/1tHF9lH.

# Notes

## Prologue

1 Juan Manuel Chaves Echeverri, 'The Global Financial Tsunami: 2008,' *Lingnan Journal of Banking, Finance and Economics* (2012) Volume 3, http://bit.ly/1tHFaGe.

Hank Paulson, 'On the Brink: Inside the Race to Stop the Collapse of the Global Financial System,' *Business Plus*, February 2010.

Ashley Seager, Jill Treanor and Patrick Wintour, 'Staring into the abyss,' *Guardian*, October 8, 2008, accessed January 22, 2014. http://bit.ly/1tHF9lF.

2 Satoshi Nakamoto, 'Bitcoin: A Peer-to-Peer Electronic Cash System,' August 31, 2008, http://bit.ly/1tHFaWK.

3 Satoshi Nakamoto, 'Bitcoin P2P e-cash paper,' Cryptography Mailing List, November 1, 2008, accessed March 2, 2014. http://bit.ly/1tHF9lM.

4 Ibid.

5 SourceForge.net, accessed January 22, 2014, http://bit.ly/1tHFbtP.

# What is Bitcoin? How is it Made?

6 New Liberty Standard, '2009 Exchange Rate,' accessed January 28, 2014, http://bit.ly/1tHFbtR.

7 American Time Use Survey, BLS, October 23, 2013, accessed May 8, 2014, http://1.usa.gov/1tHFbtU.

8 Asli Demirguc-Kunt and Leora Klapper, 'Measuring Financial Inclusion: The Global Findex Database,' World Bank, April 1, 2012, http://bit.ly/1tHF9lS.

9 'How Currency Gets into Circulation,' Federal Reserve Bank of New York, February 7, 2014, http://nyfed.org/1tHF8OC.

10 Based on US M3 (one measure of money supply) of $16 trillion, Nick Laird, 'Sharelynx,' February 10, 2014, http://bit.ly/1tHF9lT. Based on M2 (another money supply measure) of $11 trillion, about 11% of US dollars exist in physical form, Federal Reserve Bank of St Louis, February 10, 2014, http://bit.ly/1tHF8OH.

11 'How Currency Gets into Circulation,' Federal Reserve Bank of New York, February 7, 2014, http://nyfed.org/1tHF8OC.

12 Bank of England Statistical Release, January 30, 2014, accessed February 10, 2014, http://bit.ly/1tHF7KB.

13 Satoshi Nakamoto, 'Bitcoin open source implementation of P2P currency,' P2P Foundation, accessed January 28, 2014, http://bit.ly/1tHFaWL.

14 Ibid.

15 David Chaum. 'Blind signatures for untraceable

payments,' 1982, accessed February 13, 2014, http://bit.ly/1tHFaGd.

16 'How DigiCash Blew Everything,' Next, January 1999, accessed February 11, 2014, http://bit.ly/1tHF9C8.

17 Stephen Foley, 'Bitcoin needs to learn from past e-currency failures,' Financial Times, November 28, 2013, accessed February 11, 2014, http://on.ft.com/1tHFaGn.

18 'Bitcoin open source implementation of P2P currency.'

19 Gwern Branwen, 'Silk Road: Theory & Practice' June 2011, accessed May 14, 2014. bit.ly/1tHF8y9.

20 'Bitcoin open source implementation of P2P currency.'

21 Leslie Lamport, Robert Shostak and Marshall Pease, 'The Byzantine Generals Problem,' SRI International, April 1980. *Reliable computer systems must handle malfunctioning components that give conflicting information to different parts of the system. This situation can be expressed abstractly in terms of a group of generals of the Byzantine army camped with their troops around an enemy city. Communicating only by messenger, the generals must agree upon a common battle plan. However, one or more of them may be traitors who will try to confuse the others. The problem is to find an algorithm to ensure that the loyal generals will reach agreement. It is shown that, using only oral messages, this problem is solvable if and only if more than two-thirds of the generals are loyal; so a single traitor can confound two loyal generals.*

22 'Bitcoin open source implementation of P2P currency.'

23 Gwern Branwen, 'Silk Road: Theory & Practice,' June 2011, accessed May 14, 2014, http://bit.ly/1tHF8y9.

24 Joshua Davis, 'The crypto-currency,' New Yorker, October 10, 2011, 62.

25 Ibid.

26 Dan Kaminsky, 'I Tried Hacking Bitcoin and I Failed,' Business Insider, April 12, 2013, accessed March 10, 2014, http://read.bi/1tHF8OE.

## The Anarchic Computing Subculture where Bitcoin has its Roots

27 Tim May, 'The Crypto Anarchist Manifesto,' 1998, accessed March 3, 2014. http://bit.ly/1tHF8OI.

28 Eric Hughes, 'A cypherpunk's manifesto,' March 1993, accessed January 27, 2014, http://bit.ly/1tru7gG.

29 Ibid.

30 Before Bitcoin was announced, Satoshi contacted Adam Back, wanting to make sure he was referencing Back correctly. In their exchange, Back said Satoshi's idea reminded him of Dai's. Satoshi then emailed Dai, saying, 'I was very interested to read your b-money page. I'm getting ready to release a paper that expands on your ideas into a complete working system. Adam Back (Hashcash.org) noticed the similarities and pointed me to your site.' It's possible Satoshi had had the same idea independently but was only referencing that Dai had had the idea first.

Wei Dai, comments on 'Bitcoins are not digital greenbacks', Less Wrong, April 19, 2013, accessed March 13, 2013, http://bit.ly/1tru4RU.

31 Nick Szabo, 'Bit gold,' Unenumerated, December 29, 2005, accessed March 30, 2014, http://bit.ly/1tHF95d. N.B. The earliest example I can find of Szabo's proposal dates to 2005, long before Bitcoin, and he begins his blogpost with the line, 'A long time ago I hit upon the idea of bit gold,' and there are references to it from many contemporaries, so I can see no reason to doubt the assertion that the idea was hatched in the late 1990s.

32 Morgan E. Peck, 'The Cryptoanarchists Answer to Cash,' IEEE Spectrum, May 30, 2012, accessed May,10, 2014, http://bit.ly/1tHFaWR.

33 'Bit gold.'

34 Ian Grigg, Ian Goldberg, David Chaum, Stefan Brands, Steve Schear, John Gilmore, Ryan Lackey, Ben Laurie, Jim McCoy, Bram Cohen, Paul Kocher, Zooko, Adam Shostack, Len Sassaman, Ulf Moeller and the army of cryptographers, from Gavin Andresen to Jeff Garzik and beyond, who helped develop Bitcoin in the open-source community.

35 Satoshi Nakamoto, 'Bitcoin v0.1 released', Cryptography Mailing List, January 9, 2009, accessed March 2, 2014, http://bit.ly/1tru7wY.

36 Hal Finney, 'Bitcoin v0.1 released', Cryptography Mailing List. January 11, 2009, accessed March 2, 2014. http://bit.ly/1tru7wZ.

37 'Bitcoin open source implementation of P2P currency,'

## The Rise of Bitcoin and the Disappearance of its Maker

38 'Wikileaks contact info?,' BitcoinTalk, Novem-

ber–December, 2010, accessed March 23, 2014, http://bit.ly/1r'/aJg3.

39 Keir Thomas, 'Could the Wikileaks Scandal Lead to New Virtual Currency?,' PC World, December 10, 2010, accessed February 26, 2014. http://bit.ly/1tHF95n.

40 'Money Laundering Using New Payment Methods,' Financial Action Taskforce, October 2010, accessed May 10, 2014, http://bit.ly/1tHFaGm.

41 Satoshi Nakamoto, 'Added some DoS limits, removed safe mode (0.3.19),' BitcoinTalk, December 12, 2010, accessed March 24, 2014, http://bit.ly/1trBfth.

42 The Bitcoin Show with Bruce Wagner, September 15, 2011, accessed February 26, 2014, http://bit.ly/1trBch2.

43 Jerry Brito, 'Online Cash Bitcoin Could Challenge Governments, Banks,' Time, April 16, 2011, accessed February 24, 2014, http://ti.me/1tru7x1.

44 'Bitcoin Virtual Currency: Unique Features Present Distinct Challenges for Deterring Illicit Activity,' United States Federal Bureau of Investigation, April 24, 2014, accessed May 15, 2014, http://wrd.cm/1tru4RX.

45 JJ Colao, 'With 60 Million Websites, WordPress Rules The Web. So Where's The Money?,' Forbes, September 5, 2012, accessed February 26, 2014, http://onforb.es/1tru7x6.

46 'Proof of massive fraudulent trading activity at Mt. Gox, and how it has affected the price of Bitcoin,' The Willy Report, May 25, 2014, accessed May 27, 2014, http://bit.ly/1tru4RY.

47 'Russian authorities say Bitcoin illegal,' Reuters, February 9, 2014, accessed February 27, 2014, http://reut.rs/1tHFaWV.

48 Robert Peston, 'Bitcoin's life-or-death moment,' BBC News, February 25, 2014, accessed February 26, 2014, http://bbc.in/1tHF8OS.

49 James Titcomb, 'Bitcoin under threat as MtGox goes offline,' Daily Telegraph, February 25, 2014, accessed February 26, 2014, http://bit.ly/1tHF9lC.

50 mtreme, 'Gox horror story thread,' Reddit, accessed May 10, 2014, http://bit.ly/1tru7x8.

51 AdamSC1, 'Vault of Satoshi Launches Full Public Proof of Solvency (Not Just an Audit),' Reddit, April 21, 2014, accessed May 11, 2014, http://bit.ly/1tru7x9.

## Nerds, Squats and Millionaires

52 I didn't know it at the time, but Sean's Outpost is a nine-acre sanctuary for the homeless in Florida funded by bitcoin donations. It is known as Satoshi Forest.

53 Victoria McNally, 'How the Heck Do You Pronounce "Doge," Anyway?,' GeekoSystem, accessed February 10, 2014, http://bit.ly/1tHF8OJ.

## How a Computer Nerd became the FBI's Most Wanted Drug Dealer

54 David Kushner, 'Dead End on Silk Road: Internet Crime Kingpin Ross Ulbricht's Big Fall,' Rolling Stone, February 4, 2014, accessed March 1, 2014, http://rol.st/1tHFaGu.

55 Patrick Howell O'Neill, 'How big is the Internet's most notorious black market?,' The Daily Dot, July 30, 2013, accessed May 14, 2014, http://bit.ly/1tHF8ON.

56 Fran Berkman, 'Alleged Silk Road Mastermind Was a Dirty Hippie, Best Friend Says,' Mashable, November 4, 2013, accessed March 1, 2014, http://on.mash.to/1tHF8y5.

57 Ibid.

58 Ross Ulbricht, 'Thoughts on Freedom,' July 6, 2010, accessed March 1, 2014, http://on.fb.me/1trBch6.

59 Adam Taylor, 'Alleged Founder Of Silk Road Posted LinkedIn Manifesto About Using Economic Theory To Change The World,' Business Insider, October 2, 2013, accessed March 1, 2014, http://read.bi/1tHFbds.

60 Fran Berkman, 'Alleged Silk Road Mastermind Was a Dirty Hippie, Best Friend Says,' Mashable, November 4, 2013, accessed March 1, 2014, http://on.mash.to/1tHF8y5.

61 'Anonymous market online?,' Shroomery, January 27, 2011, accessed March 1, 2014, http://bit.ly/1tru4S2.

62 'Huge sell off + Ordering not possible on MtGox', BitcoinTalk, June 19, 2011, accessed March 1, 2014, http://bit.ly/1tru4S5.

63 'IT pro needed for venture backed bitcoin startup,' BitcoinTalk, October 11, 2011, accessed March 1, 2014, http://bit.ly/1tru7xg.

64 Ulbricht Criminal Complaint. FBI Agent Christopher Tarbell before Honorable Frank Maas, United States Magistrate Judge, Southern District of New York, October 2013, accessed March 1, 2014, http://bit.ly/1tru7xf.

65 Ibid.

66 Ibid.

67 Ibid.

68 Ibid.

69 Ibid.

70 David Gilbert, 'FBI's Christopher Tarbell – The Elliot Ness of Cyberspace who Busted Silk Road,' International Business Times, October 3, 2013, accessed March 2, 2014, http://bit.ly/1tHF8yl.

71 'DarkList Aims To Be The 'Yelp' Of Silk-Road-Style Drug Dealers,' Mainstreamlos, January 24, 2014, accessed February 28, 2014, http://bit.ly/1tru4S7.

72 Ibid.

## Who is Satoshi Nakamoto?

73 Leah McGrath Goodman, 'The Face Behind Bitcoin,' Newsweek, March 6, 2014, http://bit.ly/1tHFaGp.

74 Dorian Nakamoto, 'Reviews,' Amazon, accessed March 11, 2014 http://amzn.to/1tru7Nv.

75 Ibid.

76 Dorian Nakamoto, email message to Ann Kerman, December 1, 2009, accessed April 10, 2014. http://bit.ly/1tru7Nw.

77 O Scale Trains Magazine, July/August 2009, 19, accessed April 10, 2014, http://bit.ly/1truasE.

78 Satoshi Nakamoto, comment on 'Bitcoin open source

implementation of P2P currency,' P2P Foundation, March 7, 2014, accessed March 11, 2014. http://bit.ly/1tru7Nx.

79 Andrew Smith, Twitter, accessed April 10, 2014, http://bit.ly/1truasF.

80 Hal Finney, 'Detecting Double Spending,' October 15, 1993, accessed February 15, 2014, http://bit.ly/1truasH.

81 'Bitcoin v0.1 released,' The Cryptography Archive, accessed January 24, 2014, http://bit.ly/1tru7Ny.

82 Satoshi Nakamoto, 'Re: Bitcoin does NOT violate Mises' Regression Theorem,' BitcoinTalk, 27 August, 2010, accessed March 3, 2014, http://bit.ly/1trBch7.

83 Hal Finney, 'Bitcoin and me,' Bitcointalk, March 19, 2013, accessed January 24, 2014, http://bit.ly/1trBftp.

84 Ibid.

85 Ibid.

86 Andy Greenberg, 'Nakamoto's Neighbor: My Hunt For Bitcoin's Creator Led To A Paralyzed Crypto Genius,' Forbes, March 25, 2013, accessed March 26, 2014, http://onforb.es/1tHF8ym.

87 'Weaknesses,' Bitcoin Wiki, accessed March 5, 2014, http://bit.ly/1trBch8.

88 Greenberg, 'Nakamoto's Neighbor: My Hunt For Bitcoin's Creator Led To A Paralyzed Crypto Genius.'

89 Ibid.

90 'Bitcoin and me.'

91 Satoshi Nakamoto, 'Re: Bitcoin P2P e-cash paper,'

Cryptography Mailing List, November 14, 2008, accessed February 19, 2013, http://bit.ly/1tru7NC.

92 Wei Dai, comments on 'Bitcoins are not digital greenbacks,' Less Wrong, April 19, 2013, accessed March 13, 2013, http://bit.ly/1tru4RU. See also: Note 30.

93 Satoshi Nakamoto, 'Re: They want to delete the Wikipedia article,' BitcoinTalk, July 20, 2010, accessed May 15, 2014, http://bit.ly/1trBcha.

94 Nick Szabo, 'Bitcoin, what took ye so long?', Unenumerated, May 28, 2011, accessed March 25, 2014, http://bit.ly/1tHFbde.

95 Gwern Branwen, 'Happy birthday, Satoshi Nakamoto,' Reddit/bitcoin, April 5, 2014, accessed May 20, 2014, http://bit.ly/1tru7ND.

96 Satoshi Nakamoto, 'Re: Bitcoin P2P e-cash paper,' Cryptography Mailing List, November 7, 2008, accessed February 19, 2013, http://bit.ly/1truasJ.

97 Ibid.

98 Satoshi Nakamoto, 'Re: Bitcoin P2P e-cash paper,' Cryptography Mailing List, November 14, 2008, accessed February 19, 2013, http://bit.ly/1tru7NC.

99 Satoshi Nakamoto, '[bitcoin-list] Bitcoin 0.3 released!,' Sourceforge, July 6, 2010, accessed May 22, 2014, http://bit.ly/1tru7NE.

100 Satoshi Nakamoto, 'Bitcoin P2P e-cash paper,' Cryptography Mailing List, November 8, 2008, accessed May 20, 2014, http://bit.ly/1truasP.

101 Satoshi Nakamoto, 'Bitcoin P2P e-cash paper,'

Cryptography Mailing List, November 8, 2008, accessed May 20, 2014, http://bit.ly/1truasP.

102 Satoshi Nakamoto, 'Bitcoin open source implementation of P2P currency,' P2P Foundation, February 11, 2009, accessed January 28, 2014, http://bit.ly/1tHFaWL.

103 Satoshi Nakamoto, 'tcatm's 4-way SSE2 for Linux 32/64-bit is in 0.3.10,' BitcoinTalk, August 19, 2010, accessed March 5, 2014, http://bit.ly/1trBchb.

104 Satoshi Nakamoto, 'tcatm's 4-way SSE2 for Linux 32/64-bit is in 0.3.10,' BitcoinTalk, August 15, 2010, accessed March 5, 2014, http://bit.ly/1trBfts.

105 Satoshi Nakamoto, 'tcatm's 4-way SSE2 for Linux 32/64-bit is in 0.3.10', BitcoinTalk, August 15, 2010, accessed March 5, 2014, http://bit.ly/1trBchd.

106 Satoshi Nakamoto, 'tcatm's 4-way SSE2 for Linux 32/64-bit is in 0.3.10,' BitcoinTalk, August 15, 2010, accessed March 5, 2014, http://bit.ly/1trBftu.

107 MoonShadow, 're. Who is Satoshi Nakamoto?,' April 18, 2011, accessed March 25, 2014, http://bit.ly/1trBftw.

108 If you're interested in pursuing this line further, start here – http://bit.ly/1tru7NH and here http://bit.ly/1tru7NI. Reading the debug.log is not easy, but you can find Finney's IP (his server still publicly runs on it, making it verifiable as his) and you can find another Californian IP which seems to be initiating the transaction, as well as a Tor-cloaked IP. Those were the only 3 IPs in the world using Bitcoin that day, and so it seems what was going on was that Finney started his client to receive the promised transaction, Satoshi was sitting in the channel with his favourite IRC client tunnelled

through Tor in order to anonymously monitor the details of the P2P networking, and then Satoshi's Bitcoin client was there to do the actual transaction (the Satoshi client did not support Tor for another year or two). Once you've understood that, see the follow up here – http://bit.ly/1tru7NK.

109 'Bitcoin and me.'

110 AnonymousSpeech.com, accessed January 22, 2014. http://bit.ly/1trBchh.

111 Satoshi Nakamoto, 'Re: IPv6, headless client, and more,'BitcoinTalk, June 27, 2010, accessed March 10, 2014, http://bit.ly/1pLBdbX.

112 Satoshi Nakamoto, 'Re. Potential Disaster Scenario,' August 15, 2010, accessed March 25, 2014, http://bit.ly/1trBfJK.

113 Satoshi Nakamoto, 'Re: wiki registration email,' July 29, 2010, accessed March 25, 2014, http://bit.ly/1trBfJN.

114 Satoshi Nakamoto, Bitcointalk, accessed February 26, 2014, http://bit.ly/1trBfJQ and http://bit.ly/1trBchl.

115 Satoshi Nakamoto, 'Re:URI-scehem for bitcoin,' BitcoinTalk, February 24, 2010, accessed March 10, 2010, http://bit.ly/1trBfJS. (N.B. 'photo it' – is that something a native English speaker would say? I guess so, possibly, just.)

116 Satoshi Nakamoto, 'Re: How fast do the fastest computers generate bitcoins?', BitcoinTalk, June 22, 2010, accessed March 10, 2014, http://bit.ly/1trBcxA.

117 Satoshi Nakamoto, 'Re: Potential Disaster Scenario,' BitcoinTalk August 15, 2010, accessed March 10, 2014. http://bit.ly/1trBcxA.

118 Satoshi Nakamoto, 'Re. Slashdot Submission for 1.0,' BitcoinTalk, July 5, 2010, accessed March 14, 2014, http://bit.ly/1tru7NL. As a side note, I'm a comedian who writes about economics and finance – in particular about money. One of the hardest disciplines I have always found is to put these subjects – especially money – in a language people understand. I rather identify with Satoshi saying it's 'bloody hard' to do this. One of my frustrations with the economics and finance is that they're often written in a language lay-people can't understand. Being a comedian you have to be understood – if the audience doesn't understand, they don't laugh and you're screwed. But there is no such pressure in the world of finance. Sometimes it actually seems to suit people to be vague. Alan Greenspan, former head of the Federal Reserve Bank, was a master obfuscator. His utterings became known as 'Fedspeak', which, he said, 'is a language of purposeful obfuscation to avoid certain questions'. Remember the famous George Orwell quote, 'The great enemy of clear language is insincerity. When there is a gap between one's real and one's declared aims, one turns as it were instinctively to long words and exhausted idioms, like a cuttlefish spurting out ink'. Orwell felt there was a link between bad prose and oppressive ideology. Anyway, Satoshi appears to be aware of this very dynamic, that clarity and transparency were essential if Bitcoin was to be successful. I do find a lot of Satoshi's posts difficult to understand – particularly when he writes about coding matters – but, on the whole, his command of English is considerably better than many native-English speaking financial commentators.

119 Gwern Branwen, comments on 'Wei Dai comments on

AALWA,' Less Wrong, March 21, 2014, accessed March 25, 2014, http://bit.ly/1tHFaGj.

120 Satoshi Nakamoto, 'Bitcoin v0.1 released,' January 16, 2009, accessed March 4, 2014, http://bit.ly/1truasU.

121 Satoshi Nakamoto, 'Re. The dollar cost of bitmining energy,' BitcoinTalk, July 16, 2010, accessed April 10, 2014, http://bit.ly/1trBcxC.

122 Satoshi Nakamoto, 'Re. Potential Disaster Scenario,' August 15, 2010, accessed March 25, 2014, http://bit.ly/1trBfJK.

123 Satoshi Nakamoto, 'Re: A few suggestions,' BitcoinTalk, December 13, 2009, accessed March 10, 2014, http://bit.ly/1trBcxE.

124 Satoshi Nakamoto, 'Re: Transactions and Scripts: DUP HASH160...EQUALVERIFY CHECKSIG,' BitcoinTalk, June 18, 2010, accessed March 5, 2014, http://bit.ly/1trBcxI.

125 Satoshi Nakamoto, 'Bitcoin open source implementation of P2P currency,' P2P Foundation, February 11, 2009, accessed February 19, 2014. http://bit.ly/1tru84o.

126 Satoshi Nakamoto Profile, P2P Foundation, accessed February 19, 2014, http://bit.ly/1tru841.

127 Satoshi Nakamoto, 'Bitcoin P2P e-cash paper,' Cryptography Mailing List, November 1, 2008, accessed March 2, 2014, http://bit.ly/1tHF9lM.

128 Michael J. Casey, 'Bitcoin Foundation's Andresen on Working with Satoshi Nakamoto,' Wall Street Journal, March 6, 2014, accessed March 10, 2014, http://on.wsj.com/1tHF8yc.

129 Bitcoin Wiki, accessed February 19, 2014, https://en.bitcoin.it//Satoshi_Nakamoto.

130 Bitcoin Wiki, accessed February 19, 2014, https://en.bitcoin.it//Satoshi_Nakamoto.

131 Steve, 'Who is Satoshi Nakamoto,' Bitcointalk Forums, April 18, 2011, accessed February 20, 2014, http://bit.ly/1trBcxQ.

132 Wei Dai, comments on 'AALWA: Ask any LessWronger anything,' Less Wrong, 17 March 2014, accessed March 25, 2013. http://bit.ly/1tHFaGj.

133 Greenberg, 'Nakamoto's Neighbor: My Hunt For Bitcoin's Creator Led To A Paralyzed Crypto Genius.'

134 Ibid.

135 Wei Dai, comments on 'AALWA: Ask any LessWronger anything,' Less Wrong, 17 March 2014, accessed March 25, 2013. http://bit.ly/1tHFaGj.

136 Regarding Adam Back, consider also his first post at BitcoinTalk in April 2013. '*Oh the ignominy of it. Hi, I am Adam Back, inventor of Hashcash (the bitcoin mining function). I also implemented the opensource library credlib which implements Chaum and Brands ecash. I consulted for Nokia on ecash crypto back in 2002. I worked at Zero-Knowledge Systems from 2000-2003. So anyway I know a few things about ecash, privacy tech, crypto, distributed systems (my comp sci PhD is in distributed systems) and I guess I was one of the moderately early people to read about and try to comprehend the p2p crypto cleverness that is bitcoin...If like Hal Finney I'd actually tried to run the miner back then, I may too be sitting on some genesis/bootstrap era coins. Alas I own not a single bitcoin.*'

Adam Back, "Re. Introduce yourself :)," BitcoinTalk, April 18, 2013, accessed February 19, 2014, http://bit.ly/1trBfK0. Reading through his posts at BitcoinTalk in 2013, it's clear he was learning about Bitcoin. It's hard to fake a learning curve and I doubt Satoshi would have bothered. Back has given several interviews about Bitcoin and his insight is vast. But he missed the Bitcoin train when it left the station. He is not Satoshi.

137 Wei Dai, comments on 'Bitcoins are not digital greenbacks,' Less Wrong, 19 April, 2013, accessed March 13, 2013, http://bit.ly/1tru4RU.

138 Wei Dai, comments under 'Making Money with Bitcoin,' 25 February, 2011, accessed March 12, 2014, http://bit.ly/1truaJb.

139 Graduation database, accessed May 1, 2014, http://bit.ly/1tru843.

140 Nick Szabo, 'Increasing subscriber base,' Cypherpunks Mailing List, November 1, 1993, accessed March 12, 2014, http://bit.ly/1tru847.

141 Nicholas Szabo, 'Shelling Out – On The Origins Of Money,' 2002, accessed April 10, 2014, http://bit.ly/1tHFbdp.

142 Satoshi Nakamoto, 're. Bitcoins are most like shares of common stock,' BitcoinTalk, August 20, 2010, accessed March 4, 2014, http://bit.ly/1oos0FD.

143 Nick Szabo, 'Bit gold markets,' Unenumerated, April 8, 2008, accessed March 11, 2014, http://bit.ly/1tHF95b.

144 Nick Szabo, 'Re: on anonymity, identity, reputation, and

spoofing,' Cypherpunks Mailing List, October 18, 1993, accessed March 29, 2014, http://bit.ly/1truaJg.

145 Skye Grey, 'Like In A Mirror,' accessed March 26, 2013, http://likeinamirror.wordpress.com.

146 Skye Grey, 'Occam's Razor: who is most likely to be Satoshi Nakamoto?', Like In A Mirror, March 11, 2014, accessed April 1, 2014, http://bit.ly/1tHFaGq.

147 Gwern Branwen, comment on 'Satoshi Nakaoto is (probably) Nick Szabo,' Reddit, December 1, 2013, accessed March 30, 2014, http://bit.ly/1tru849.

148 Adam L. Penenberg, 'The Bitcoin Crypto-Currency Mystery Reopened,' Fast Company, October 11, 2011, accessed May 20, 2014, http://bit.ly/1tHF8OR.

149 Satoshi Nakamoto, email message to Wei Dai, 'Re. Citation of your b-money page,' January 10, 2009, accessed May 22, 2014, http://bit.ly/1truaJj.

150 'Researchers uncover likely author of original Bitcoin paper,' Aston University, April 16, 2014, accessed May 15, 2014, http://bit.ly/1tHFaWU.

151 Nick Szabo, Keynote speech on smart contracts (presented at the IEEE International Workshop on Electronic Contracting (WEC), San Diego, California, USA, July 6, 2004), accessed April 10, 2014, http://bit.ly/1tru84a.

152 Nick Szabo, 'New Zealander challenges Amazon one-click patent,' Unenumerated, December 20, 2005, accessed March 12, 2014, http://bit.ly/1tHF95j.

153 Nick Szabo, 'Contracts With Bearer,' 1997, 1999, accessed April 10, 2014, http://bit.ly/1truaJk.

154 Nick Szabo, 'Consulting Services,' Unenumerated, April 2, 2008, accessed March 30, 2014, http://bit.ly/1tHF95e.

155 Satoshi Nakamoto, 'Re. Slashdot Submission for 1.0,' BitcoinTalk, July 5, 2010, accessed March 14, 2014, http://bit.ly/1tru7NL.

156 Nick Szabo, 'Bit gold', Unenumerated, December 29, 2005, accessed March 30, 2014, http://bit.ly/1truaJm.

157 Nick Szabo, 'Flying Money,' Unenumerated, August 27, 2008, accessed March 30, 2014, http://bit.ly/1tHF95h.

158 Nick Szabo, 'Antiques, time, gold, and bit gold,' Unenumerated, August 28, 2008, accessed April 1, 2014, http://bit.ly/1tHFbdq.

159 Satoshi Nakamoto, 'Bitcoin open source implementation of P2P currency', P2P Foundation February 11, 2009, accessed March 30, 2014. http://bit.ly/1tru84o.

160 'Bit gold.',

161 Ibid.

162 'Bitcoin open source implementation of P2P currency.'

163 Nick Szabo, 'Ten ways to make a political difference,' Unenumerated, August 12, 2007, accessed May 22, 2014, http://bit.ly/1tHF95l.

164 Nick Szabo, 'Ben Bernanke plays John Law,' Unenumerated, May 13, 2008, accessed May 22, 2014, http://bit.ly/1tHFaXo.

165 Hal Finney, 'Re. Bitcoin P2P ecash paper,' Cryptography Mailing List, November 8, 2008, http://bit.ly/1trvGLt.

166 Satoshi Nakamoto, 'They want to delete the Wikipedia

article,' BitcoinTalk, July 20, 2010, accessed March 30, 2014, http://bit.ly/1trBcha.

167 Gwern Branwen, 'Bitcoin is worse is better,' Gwern.net, May 27, 2011, accessed April 1, 2014. http://bit.ly/1tHF7KL.

168 Andrew Smith, 'Desperately seeking Satoshi,' The Sunday Times, March 2, 2014, http://thetim.es/1trvlD1

169 Adrian Chen, Twitter, accessed April 1, 2014, http://bit.ly/1trBcO7.

## Why Bitcoin is the Enemy of the State

170 Steve Connor, 'Flu epidemic traced to Great War transit camp,' The Irish Independent, January 8, 2000, accessed February 1, 2014, http://bit.ly/1tHF8yf.

171 Alan Greenspan, US Federal Reserve Board's semi-annual Monetary Policy Report to the US Congress, February 11, 2004.

172 E.C. Riegel, 'The New Approach to Freedom', Chapter 3, The Heather Foundation, 2003, http://bit.ly/1tHF956.

173 Michael McLeay, Amar Radia, Ryland Thomas, 'Money creation in the modern economy', Bank of England Quarterly Bulletin, Q1 2014.

174 Dominic Frisby, Life After the State (London, Unbound, 2013).

175 'National Average Wage Index 2012,' US Social Security Administration, accessed March 17, 2014, http://1.usa.gov/1t7vGLy.

176 The average UK wage has gone from around from £2,000 per annum in 1971 to around £25,000 in 2014.

177 The most obvious form of consumption tax, and the hardest to hide, is to tax use of the land – land value tax. Its proponents argue that it would also bring about the much needed re-balancing of land ownership. Seventy per cent of the UK, for example, is owned by 0.7% of the people – and they receive subsidy for it. A world in which they have to pay tax on that land, instead of receiving subsidy for it, would see many sell land they are not making use of because it has become a liability rather than an asset.

178 Satoshi Nakamoto, 'Re: Bitcoin P2P e-cash paper,' Cryptography Mailing List, November 14, 2008, accessed March 17, 2014, http://bit.ly/1tru7NC.

## How Bitcoin will Change the World

179 Tim Worstall, 'Finally, A Proper Use For Bitcoin, Avoiding Capital Controls,' Forbes, November 21, 2013, accessed May 25, 2014, http://onforb.es/1tHFbtQ.

180 Tyler Durden, 'JPMorgan On The Inevitability Of Europe-Wide Capital Controls,' Zero Hedge, March 22, 2013, accessed March 15, 2014, http://bit.ly/1tHFaGl.

181 Jon Southurst, 'Why China is Leading the Global Rise of Bitcoin,' Coindesk, November 18, 2013, accessed March 19, 2014, http://bit.ly/1tHF957.

182 'Credit Card Ownership Statistics,' Statistic Brain, July 24, 2012, accessed March 17, 2014, http://bit.ly/1tHFaGg.

183 'Number of credit card holders fell in India: HSBC

survey,' The Hindu Business Line, May 13, 2013, accessed March 20, 2014, http://bit.ly/1tHFaWP.

182 'All About Bitcoin,' Top Of Mind, Issue 21, Goldman Sachs Global Investment Research, March 11, 2014, http://bit.ly/1tHF8hR.

183 'Squawk Box,' CNBC, March 14, 2014, accessed March 17, 2014, http://cnb.cx/1tHF7KJ.

185 Ibid.

187 'All About Bitcoin.'

188 Ibid.

189 Ibid.

190 Kyla Yeoman, 'M-Pesa helps world's poorest go to the bank using mobile phones,' Christian Science Monitor, January 6, 2014, accessed March 15, 2014, http://bit.ly/1tHF9lH.

191 Ibid.

192 NBC News, 'Cell phones could "completely change the livelihood of many Kenyans"', August 8, 2012, accessed April 10, 2014, http://nbcnews.to/1tHFaGc

193 Kyla Yeoman, 'M-Pesa helps world's poorest go to the bank using mobile phones,' Christian Science Monitor, January 6, 2014, accessed March 15, 2014, http://bit.ly/1tHF9lH.

194 Census of India 2011.

195 Sudeep Jain, 'Why So Few Indians Have Bank Accounts,' Wall Street Journal India, November 1, 2012, accessed March 15, 2014, http://on.wsj.com/1tHFaGt.

196 Ibid.

## Should You Buy In?

197 All of these calculations assume all 21 million coins have been mined. If they haven't, the targets will be higher.

## Appendix II: Who Is Satoshi? The Usual Suspects

198 'Interview with Jed McCaleb, inventor of the Ripple protocol and co-founder of OpenCoin,' Ripple, April 17, 2013, accessed March 12, 2014, http://bit.ly/1tHF8OD.

199 Ibid.

200 Jed McCaleb, 'Hiring C++ and JS programmers,' BitcoinTalk, September 11, 2012, accessed March 11, 2014. http://bit.ly/1CNGtWX.

201 Michael J. Casey, 'Bitcoin Foundation's Andresen on Working with Satoshi Nakamoto,' Wall Street Journal, March 6, 2014, accessed March 10, 2014, http://on.wsj.com/1tHF8yc.

202 'Occam's Razor: who is most likely to be Satoshi Nakamoto?'.

# Subscribers

Dear Reader,

The book you are holding came about in a rather different way to most others. It was funded directly by readers through a new website: Unbound.

Unbound is the creation of three writers. We started the company because we believed there had to be a better deal for both writers and readers. On the Unbound website, authors share the ideas for the books they want to write directly with readers. If enough of you support the book by pledging for it in advance, we produce a beautifully bound special subscribers' edition and distribute a regular edition and e-book wherever books are sold, in shops and online.

This new way of publishing is actually a very old idea (Samuel Johnson funded his dictionary this way). We're just using the internet to build each writer a network of patrons. Here, at the back of this book, you'll find the names of all the people who made it happen.

Publishing in this way means readers are no longer just passive consumers of the books they buy, and authors are free to write the books they really want. They get a much fairer return too – half the profits their books generate, rather than a tiny percentage of the cover price.

If you're not yet a subscriber, we hope that you'll want to

join our publishing revolution and have your name listed in one of our books in the future. To get you started, here is a £5 discount on your first pledge. Just visit unbound.com, make your pledge and type BUCCMASTER5 in the promo code box when you check out.

Thank you for your support,

Dan, Justin and John
Founders, Unbound

William Bonner
Ron Bowd
James Branch
Jean Branch
David Brand
Peter Brand
Micah Brandon
Jordi Bravo Canales
Toby Bray
Dean Browell
Richard Buchanan
Chris Bull
Anthony Bunge
Paul Burgess
Russell Burns
Jackie Bussey
Gordon Butler
James Butterworth
Stephen Calnan
D Campbell
Andrew Campling
Peter Capper
Neil Carbarns
Francesco Carbone
Eamonn Carey
Philip Carr
Chloe & Greg Carter
Steve Carter
    Be-Printed.co.uk
Lucas Casado Lausin
Piers Caswell

Sebastian Chambers
Jay Chmelauskas
Jarred Christmas
I Churchward
Pete Clark
Kate Clemens
Andrew Clive
Philip Cockayne
Matthew Cocking
Michael Cohee
Nicholas Cohn
CoinDesk
CoinScrum CoinScrum
Ady Coles
Jeremy Coles
Rob Coles
Stevyn Colgan
Mike Colvin
Myles Cooney
Paul Cooper
Roderick Corrie
Leonardo A. Cosio
Michael Coulson
Steve Court
Paula Cousins
Jason Cozens
John Crawford
Mark Cross
J. Greg Crumpton /
    AirTight.co / Est. 1999
Alan Cunnane

Damien Daly

Howard Daniel

Geoffrey Darnton

Callum Davey

Keith Davey

Keith Davidson

Jane Davies

Jonathan Davis

Mike Davis

Floyd DCosta

Jean-Francois De Rudder

Lykle de Vries – @lykle

Rupert Degas

Gary Delaney

A Dickson

Gordon Dinnage

Nick Divehall

Simon Dixon

Iain Docherty

Noel Doherty

Sean Donaghey

Kevin Donnellon

Christine Doppelt

Kevin Dowd

Daniel Diginoise
    Drozdzewski

Gordon Duncan

Joe Durak

Amanda Durham

Tim Durham

Mag. Dr. Helgo Eberwein

Michi Eder

Malcolm Edwards

Terry Egalton

Scott Elliott-Brand

Chris Emery

Dorothy Emery

Willie Evans

Nigel Everett

Michael Fabbri

Mike Fallbrown

Mick Farrell

Jane Farrelly

Paul Faux

Joe Feser

Paul Fisher

Rob Fisher

Bill Foord

Derek Forrest

Simon Foster

John George Fothergill

Nicholas Fox

Luca Franco

Isobel Frankish

Andrew French

Terence Frisby

Mark Fry

Sara Galbraith

Andrew Gamble

Mark Gamble

Richard Ganley

Sherman Garner

Alistair Geddes
Steve Geddes
Robert V Gerhardt
Jean Germain
Mark Gibaud
Douglas Gibb
Giles Gibbons
Paulo Glorias
Pauline Godfrey
Alejandro González
Héctor Gonzalez Mila
Wooi Lynn Goon
Denise Gorse
Philip Gosling
Terence Gould
Noel Graham
Justin Grainger
Angus Grant
John Grant
Paul Green
Mark Greening
Darren Griffin
Alex Griffiths
Mike Griffiths
Neil Grosse
Judith Gunton
Babette Haag
Keith Hackwell
Salim Halabi
Duncan Hannay Robertson
Diane Hannon

Susan Harper
Andrew Hart
Jon Hather
Charlotte Hauser
Eizabeth Head
Jack Healy
Andrew Hearse
Mark Helyer
Andrew Hemingway
Marc Henderson
Sally Higgens
David Hillier
Chris Hoare
Samuel Hoban
Diana Hobart
Derek Hodge
Raymond Hodgkinson
Tim Hodgkiss
Paul Hoffmeister
Mathias Holm
Carl Holt
Robert Hookway
Darren Hopkinson
Vic Hough
Mick Howarth
Matthew Hudson
Darren Hughes
Haley Hughes
James Hughes
Ken Hunnisett
Philip Hunter

Ian Hutchinson
Neil Hutchinson
Musa Ismail
Mohamad Issa
(www.linkedin.com/in/
issao5)
John Jakeways
Paul Jenneson
Giles Jerrit
Ismail Johari
James Johnson
Alan Johnston
Chris Jones
Justine Jones
Barry Jordan
John Jordan
Rene Jørgensen
Walter Kabai
Wendy Keenan
David Kelly
John Kelly
Shaun Keogh
Gordon Kerr
Andy Kimpton-Nye
Laszlo Kiralyfi
Mark Kirkham
James Knight
Katie Knight
Leaksmy Kong
Tomi Kovanen

Laurent Kssis – Crypto &
ETFs Funds!
Dave Lang
Paul Laviers
Tricia Lawlor
Julian Lawrence
W Tom Lawrie
John Lawton
Peter Le Morvan
Jimmy Leach
Paul Leaver
Richard Lee
Adrian Lewis
Erik Løgstrup
Mr London – Paul Harrison
Connie Lopes
Anthony Lorkin
Jeremy Lysaght
Iain Maccallum
George McClure
Ross Mcdonald
Neil Macehiter
Robert McIntosh
James MacKenzie
Gavin McKeown
Ian McLeod
Clinton Madgwick
Dale MADinMelbourne
Hedy Manders
Matt Manhattan
Nathan Marley

Dominick Marshall-Smith
Lee Mascall
Robert Masding
Robert Maskell
Paul Maskens
David Maslin
Ronald Matsushige
Philip Matthew
William Matthews
David Maxwell-Lyte
Elizabeth Stella Maria
   Mellen
Brian Micklethwait
Anthony Milas
Peter Milburn
Don Miller
Peter Mitchell
Alexandru Mitoi
Greg Moffitt
Richard Montagu
Richard Morrin
Andrew Morris
Charlie Morris
Chris Morris
Luke Morris
Ed Morron
Andrew Morton
Chris Mounsey
Pete Moyer
Zingisile Castro Mtsutsa

Ronald Mulder –
   @ronaldmulder
Captain Munchkin of the
   Bridge Trolls
Simon Munns
Milosz Muszynski
Bandish Nayee
Ghassan Nehaili
Charles Newsome
Colin Nicholson
Ian Nicholson
James Noble
Keith Noble
Padraic Noonan
Andrew Nowson
Matthew Noyes
Jefferson Nunn
Toonna Obi-Okoye
Mark O'Byrne
Jerry O'Callaghan
Kath O'Donnell
Neil O'Donnell
Edward Kevin O'Hara
Irwin Olian
John Oliver
Juan Matías Olmos
Ina O' Murchu
John Orley
Arber Pacarada
Jim Page
Thomas Parker

Richard Parsons
Tony Partington
Rima Patel
Steve Pavis
Jon Pearson
Ben Pender
Larry Pesavento
Jakob Peterson – Digital
    Currency Project
Marco Pieters
Marialuisa Plassmann
Robert Pocock
Andy Polaine
Duane Poliquin
Justin Pollard
Edmund Pooh & Jenny Pooh
Julian Power
Eugenio Pozzo
David Prew
Adrian Price
Anthony Pye-Jeary
Brady Rafuse
Amanda Railson
Hans Rasmussen
RoseMary Rattray
Mark Reed
Jan Rees
Modwenna Rees-Mogg
Alex Reid
Chris Reid
Jason Reid

John R Reid
William Reid
Tamsin Rickeard
Tom Robinson
Filip Roose
Neil Ross Russell
Charles Rother
Deborah Rothwell
Graham Rowan
George Rowing
Elizabeth Rowlands
Chris Roy
John Roycroft
Linda Rumble
Benjamin Russell
Alfred Samasoni
Roger Sambrook
Seb Sander
Marnu Schm
Bob Schofield
Richard Scrase
Matthew Searle
Charles Seymour-Cole
Nicholas Sharples
Alex Shaw
John Shore
Terry Sims
Melanie Sinclair
Graham Singleton
Nick Sizer
David Skey

Kenneth Smalley
Billy Smith
David Smith
Dean L Smith
Graham Smith
James Smith
Pat Smith
Robert Smith
Ryan Smith
Scott Smith
Wade Smith
David Smith VSS
John Smithies
Dominic Snow
Princess Snozall of the River Pixies
Stuart Southall
Colin Speirs
Chris Squire
Joerg Standfuss
Clive Standish-White
Tony Stanmore
Kostadin Stoilov
Nick Stoneman
James Sturgeon
Damian Sweeney
Emilia Tai
Graham Tanker
Ezra Tassone
Chris Taylor
Jamie Taylor

Jeremy Tetlow
The Bitcoin Rat
Ulf V Thoene
Andrew Thomas
Graham Thomas
Piers Thomas
Dave Thompson
Gary Thompson
Steve Thompson
Daniel Thorley
Jan Thorskov
David Tickle
Alan Tonkin
Kieran Topping
Tony Tornquist
Michael Town
Mike Tucker
Jari Tuomola
James Turk
Demian Turner
Jeremy Tyzack
Łukasz Łakomy
Mike Valiant
Chris Vallé
Udo van den Heuvel
To Douchess Sandra Van Der Buhen
Lawrence van Kampen-Brooks
Wim Van Raemdonck
Christian van Zijl

Mark Vent

Anne Ventura

Chris Vezey

Brian Vickery

Olivier Vigneresse

James Vincent

Thomas Visegrady

Dirk vom Lehn

Chris von Koss

Gary Wales

Antony Ward

Martin Ward

Ansgar Warner

Eliot Watkins

Ian Watson

Mathew Watson

Emanuella Watson-Gandy

William Waugh

Jonathan Westwood

Jody Wetton

Peter Wiggins

Peter Wilkins

Daniel Williams

Alan Wilson

Todd Wilson

Tobias Wißmann

Danny Wolfson

Rupert Wood

Steve Woodward

Michael Woolley

Julian Wooster

Guy Wright

Will Wwift

David Wyness

Patrick Young

Daniel Zipay

# A Note About the Typeface

The body of this book is set in the Sorts Mill Goudy typeface, created by designer Barry Schwartz (b. 1961).

It is a revival of the Goudy Old Style typeface, originally created by Frederic W. Goudy (1865–1947) in 1915 for American Type Founders, the dominant American manufacturer of metal type from the late nineteenth century up until the middle of the twentieth.

Goudy himself did not train as a designer of type until he reached his forties, when he decided to quit his job keeping the books of a Chicago estate agent and retrain. Over the following 36 years, Goudy would become feverishly prolific, creating 113 fonts – more usable typefaces than some of the world's most revered type creators and punch cutters.

The 'ou' of Goudy is pronounced in the same way as the 'ou' in out, pout and gout.